Burke O. Long

The Problem of Etiological Narrative
in the Old Testament

Burke O. Long

The Problem of Etiological Narrative
in the Old Testament

Verlag Alfred Töpelmann

Berlin 1968

Beihefte zur Zeitschrift für die alttestamentliche Wissenschaft

Herausgegeben von Georg Fohrer

108

The printing of this work was made possible by a grant awarded by the trustees
of Wellesley College, through its Committee on Faculty Publications.

Preface

This monograph grew out of a chance remark some years ago, made by Brevard Childs in a seminar, that the matter of etiology needed close examination. In view of a certain impasse reached in the discussion of etiology in the Old Testament, it seemed best to focus on a limited aspect of the broader problem in the interest of building a firmer basis for informed argument. This in no way ignored the wider issues; it merely shifted the ground for further discussion, and in a way which proved to be productive. The work presented here was submitted in a slightly altered form to Yale University in candidacy for the PhD degree.

To my teachers and friends, too numerous to name, but all of whom have played a part in the production of this study, I express my sincere thanks. I am especially grateful to a friend, Dr. E. Gerstenberger, from whom I received my early and formative training, and to Prof. B. Childs, who guided with helpful and incisive criticisms each stage of this investigation. He is in no way responsible for any errors, however.

I wish to thank Prof. D. Dr. Georg Fohrer, who accepted the monograph for the *Beihefte* series, for his willing encouragement. Finally, I am deeply grateful to the trustees of Wellesley College, who provided generous financial support for the publication, as well as opportunities for stimulating study and teaching.

Burke Long

Wellesley, Massachusetts
October, 1967

Contents

Abbreviations

ANET²	Ancient Near Eastern Texts Relating to the Old Testament (2nd edition)
BASOR	Bulletin of the American Schools of Oriental Research
CAD	Chicago Assyrian Dictionary
CBQ	Catholic Biblical Quarterly
ET	English translation
EvTh	Evangelische Theologie
GK²	Gesenius' Hebrew Grammar, ed. E. Kautzsch (2nd English edition)
JAOS	Journal of the American Oriental Society
JBL	Journal of Biblical Literature
JNES	Journal of Near Eastern Studies
JSS	Journal of Semitic Studies
LXX	Septuagint
MS(S)	manuscript(s)
MT	Masoretic text
Or	Orientalia
prgr	paragraph
RB	Revue Biblique
S	Samaritan Pentateuch
SThZ	Schweizerische Theologische Zeitschrift
Suppl. VT	Supplements to Vetus Testamentum
VT	Vetus Testamentum
ZAW	Zeitschrift für die Alttestamentliche Wissenschaft
ZThK	Zeitschrift für Theologie und Kirche

Introduction

A classic definition of etiological narrative in Greek mythology as formulated by M. P. Nilsson runs:

> . . . a narrative which seeks to explain why something has come to be, or why it has become such and such[1].

This general formulation is standard and widespread, whether the literary effects are viewed with a primary interest in anthropology, comparative religion and mythology, or comparative literature[2]. The definition was early applied to Israelitic literature by Old Testament scholars[3], and has continued to be commonly accepted. Such a formulation, however, encourages the kind of negative evaluation of the historical worth of etiological tradition which A. Alt, for example, gave[4]. On the other hand, it speaks of a story's function without describing those characteristics which actually reveal its overall etiological purpose. One simply reconstructs a question — the hypothetical *Kinderfrage* — which a given myth, legend, or saga seeks to answer.

This fundamental unclarity remains in the current discussion of Old Testament etiological narrative. There are two distinct, but related questions: (a) What are the marks of etiological narrative? (b) How is a given etiological narration related to real history?

The two fold nature of the issue is often obscured. This became especially clear in the notorious disagreement between J. Bright and what he termed the "Alt-Noth School"[5]. Bright focused on the sec-

---

[1] Geschichte der griechischen Religion[2], 1941, vol. I, 25.

[2] Cf. for example, A. Lang, Myth, Ritual and Religion, 1887, vol. I, 163 ff. and passim; E. B. Tyler, Primitive Culture[2], 1873, 368 ff. Recently, A. E. Jensen, Mythos und Kult bei Naturvölkern, 1951, 91 ff. In comparative literature, cf. A. H. Krappe, The Science of Folk-Lore, 1930, 60 ff. and passim; S. Thompson, The Folktale, 1946; L. Röhrich, Märchen und Wirklichkeit[2], 1964, 27 ff.

[3] H. Gunkel, Genesis, 1901, XX—XXVI and passim. The introduction to this commentary is translated as The Legends of Genesis: The Biblical Saga and History, 1964. Cf. also H. Gressmann, Die Anfänge Israels[2], 1914, 15 f. and passim.

[4] A. Alt, Josua, now reprinted in: Kleine Schriften zur Geschichte des Volkes Israels, vol. I 1953, 176—192. Cf. especially 184 f.

[5] Early Israel in Recent History Writing: A Study in Method, 1956. Earlier, W. F. Albright, The Israelite Conquest of Canaan in the Light of Archaeology, BASOR, 74 (1939), 11—23. Bright is referring to Alt's work on Josua op. cit. and Noth's

ond question by criticizing the emphasis which the Alt-Noth school
placed on "etiology as a creative factor in the formation of tradition," and by suggesting that

> where historical traditions are concerned, not only can it be proved that the
> etiological factor is often secondary in the formation of these traditions, it cannot
> be proved that it was ever primary[6].

The question of the form critical marks of genuine etiological narrative, or even "etiological factors," and its bearing on the historian's
problem is left imprecisely formulated and almost untouched in
Bright's critique.

Noth[7] has attempted to speak to the disagreement by conceding
that genuine historical recollections might take an etiological form.
But they might not. One has to reckon, therefore, with a whole range
of probabilities. This necessitates a careful analysis of individual cases
to see whether the link between the events narrated and the phenomenon explained is genuinely historical or secondary.

At this point the other aspect of the issue emerges. According
to Noth, an "etiological interpretation" of a given narrative tradition
is justified only where certain well defined "marks" within the narrative demand it[8]. But he mentions only one such characteristic,
namely, the formula "until this day." This, of course, cannot be
used mechanically to identify etiological narrative. However, to the
extent that one remains unclear as to precisely how this sign relates
to narrative materials, and how it reveals the function of its "story"
context, and to the extent that other marks of etiological narrative
remain unexamined, the two fold issue is obscured, if not rendered
insoluble. One should mention here the review of the problem offered
by J. L. Seeligman, who attempts to clarify the concept of etiology,
and define its applicability to various Biblical materials[9].

Recently, C. Westermann has sought to clarify the matter in a
fresh way by focusing on the problem of the marks of etiological
narrative[10]. If one proceeds from his fundamental criterion for a
genuine narrative, i. e., one which describes a dramatic movement
from a tension to its resolution[11], then an etiological narrative of this
type can only be one in which the path from question — which the

---

Überlieferungsgeschichte des Pentateuch, 1948, passim. Cf. also M. Noth, Das Buch
Josua[2], 1953, passim.

[6] Bright op. cit. 91.

[7] Der Beitrag der Archäologie zur Geschichte Israels, Suppl. VT 7 (1960), 278 ff.

[8] Idem.

[9] J. L. Seeligman, Aetiological Elements in Biblical Historiography, Zion: Quarterly
for Research in Jewish History 26 (1961), 141—169 (English summary).

[10] Forschung am Alten Testament, 1964, 39—47.

[11] Derived from his analysis of "promise narratives," ibid. 18 ff.

etiology raises — to answer — which the etiological conclusion gives — coincides with the way leading from tension to resolution[12]. Thus, where one meets an etiological motif, the important question is what function it has in the wider textual unit and what this unit represents exclusive of the etiological motif[13].

My own work runs independently of Westermann's. Yet it fills out his program by attempting to define more precisely in controlled circumstances certain "etiological motifs" and how they in fact relate to the narrative material in which they appear. In a wider sense, I am speaking to the first aspect of the current discussion by searching for, and examining, repetitive "marks" of limited varieties of etiological narrative.

The investigation — limited to the material in Genesis through II Kings — seeks to define the formal structure and function of the following phrases commonly held to be etiological:

(1) Etymological clauses
  (a) "And he called (ויקרא) the (his) name so and so for he (she) said such and such."
  (b) Therefore one calls (על־כן קרא) the name (of that place) so and so.
(2) "It shall be a sign . . ." (והיה לאות).
(3) "What does such and such mean (to you)?" (מה . . . לך).

On the primary level of the history of tradition, wherever the formula appears integrally related to narrative material, the relational lines constitutive of the connection are described in a functional way. The study leads, therefore, to certain conclusions regarding the marks of narrative material which functions etiologically. Briefly, the results show that only rarely are these formulae related to a "story" complex. Thus they seldom can be used as a way of determining whether or not a given narrative served an etiological purpose.

Although these conclusions bear primarily upon the first aspect of the current discussion, namely on "marks" of etiological narrative, they also have wide implications for the historian. Apparently the creative processes reflected in the operation of the formulae never gave rise to extensive narrative tradition. This fact prohibits a quick *negative* evaluation of the historical worth of a large complex such as, for example, Jos 1—11. Thus in a limited way, the polemical caveat by J. Bright is sustained. But these conclusions also leave open the question of a *positive* evaluation, and force one to find other criteria for making a historian's judgment. In short, the form

---

[12] Ibid. 40.
[13] Ibid. 42.

critical work presented here demonstrates again the necessity for understanding in detail the nature and intent of given material as a first step toward using it as a source for historical data. This is an easily accepted requirement, but one which is often overlooked in practice.

The concluding chapter draws a few further implications for the commonly accepted way of reconstructing etiological narrative[14].

---

[14] This study was completed when two new monographs by A. Arana came to my attention: La Narración Etiológica Como Genero Literario and Las Etiologias Etimológicas del Pentateuco. These works were inaccesible to me. The summary by R. de Vaux (RB 73, 1966, 444) indicates that they do not duplicate the work presented in this monograph.

Section I
Etymological Etiologies

J. Fichtner[1] isolated two basic formulae which report the giving of a name and a reason for it. His Form I appeared in the following schema:

> And he (she) named the (his, her, or its) name (of the or that) place so and so
> For he (she, they) said: (now follows the etymological explanation for the name)

This full formula is found in Ex 2 22.

ויקרא את־שמו גרשם   β

כי אמר גר הייתי בארץ נכריה   γ

The schema occurs in this full form only rarely. Many minor variations appear. Most of the time אמר is missing and therefore *kî* introduces either a direct quotation (Gen 4 25) or an objective causal clause (Gen 3 20 26 20)[2].

Occasionally כי אמר or כי is replaced with לאמר (Gen 5 29) or with ויאמר כי (Gen 26 22)[3]. The constant elements in the form are the following:

a) The *act* of naming is *narrated* in the historical tense by the use of waw conversive prefix form of the verb *qr'* with a specific subject.

(b) The etymological explanation (γ element), with affix verb form follows the name giving itself. Occasionally a quotation or short statement which provides the motivation for the name, precedes the β element, which stands alone in such cases. The narrative force of β however, is not appreciably leasened, but is retained in the feminine verb (ותקרא). This pattern is common on the occasion of birth (e. g., Gen 29 33 30 7f. 10f. 12f.).

---

[1] J. Fichtner, Die etymologische Ätiologie in der Namengebung der geschichtlichen Bücher des Alten Testaments, VT 6 (1956), 372—396.

[2] Num 13 24 has the causal clause introduced with על אדות.

[3] Fichtner op. cit. 379.

(c) The γ element always contains a key word which is assonant with the name given. When the γ element is missing, a word play (not always assonance) is clear in an immediately preceding speech (e. g., Gen 29 33). Thus the causal relationship between the name and an event or utterance is implicit in the waw conversive form of the verb and the accompanying word play, or explicit in the full γ element.

Form II isolated by Fichtner occurs mostly according to the following schema[4]:

Therefore (על־כן) one calls the (its) name (of that place) so and so

The fundamental form is apparent in Ex 15 23:

על־כן קרא שמה מרה

In two cases this formula has been expanded by the addition of a *ki* causal clause which expresses the motivation for the particular name (Gen 11 9 21 31). This expansion may have come about through the influence of the γ elements of Form I (ויקרא . . . כי). It certainly appears to be a secondary development in the oral stages of tradition history[5].

Other variations occur as well. In one instance קרא is missing (Gen 26 33). Two passages use Niph קרא (Gen 2 23 17 5), and two show Niph אמר (Gen 22 14 32 29). Sometimes the verb קרא is modified by the adverbial (הזה) עד־היום (e. g., II Chr 20 26 Jos 7 26b Jdc 18 12). Sometimes the name itself or the place is modified by the phrase (e. g., Gen 26 33 Jdc 15 19).

The constant features of the form are as follows:

(a) Form II is always introduced by על־כן.

(b) The act of naming is not narrated. Rather, the formula expresses a logical inference from speech, reported event, or descriptive report. The link between these elements and the name is always explicit in a word play. There is a clear contrast with surrounding material, which normally relates by means of *waw* conversive *Yiqtal* verb forms a sequence of successive events. At the end point, Form II breaks the recitation with a logical inference whose function,

---

[4] Idem.

[5] This is a modification of Fichtner's assertion that Form II occurs mostly in this expanded stage. The opposite is the case. Excluding the occurrences of mixed forms, fifteen of the eighteen cases in the historical books do not show a *ki* clause. (Cf. Fichtner op. cit. 380.)

though sharing something of a narrative character at times, cannot be fully understood as simple historical narration (e. g., Jos 7 26 or II Chr 20 26). The narrative movement, as it were, ceases and a conclusion is drawn. This is the usual function of עֵל־כֵּן with a Qatal verb form in the midst of narrative prose, whether the verb has a definite or indefinite subject (definite: Gen 47 22 Jos 14 14 indefinite: I Sam 10 12. Cf. I Sam 27 6. More distant, Ex 20 11 // Dtn 5 15)[6]. Of course, the inferential function is most sharply distinguished from historical recitation where the subject of the verb is indefinite. Such is the case in most of the occurrences of Form II (cf. below).

(c) The subject of the verb is always indefinite in those cases where the verb is modified by עֵד־הַיּוֹם הַזֶּה[7] and therefore best translated by English passive, e. g., "That is why its name is called so and so . . ." The same is true in those cases in which the singular or plural pronominal subject of *qr'* cannot refer meaningfully to the agent in the immediately preceding context[8]. There remain only four cases where the subject of the verb may be definite[9]. Of these, one text (II Sam 5 20) is given a passive formulation in all Greek manuscripts, and made indefinite in the parallel passage (I Chr 14 11). All four passages are structured in a way typical of other Form II occurrences. While certainty is not possible because of the ambiguity in the Hebrew grammar, it seems likely that these four cases also must be read with an indefinite subject. In this case, the inference to a name becomes a proposition of general applicability for all times.

It happens that Form II is used almost exclusively for place name etymologies[10]. Form I, while showing a more mixed application, has an affinity for personal names[11]. Clearly, each formula is etiological. Each purports to explain the origin of a known name in terms of event, utterance, or phenomenon which is brought into a causal relationship to the giving of the name. In my opinion, the adverbial phrase עֵד־הַיּוֹם הַזֶּה seldom has anything to do with this causality.

---

[6] Occurrences of עֵל־כֵּן and Qatal verb form in speeches were excluded because they did not reflect historical narration as such. On the logical function of עֵל־כֵּן alone, cf. E. König, Historisch-kritisches Lehrgebäude der hebräischen Sprache, 1895, vol. II/1, 327, and vol. II/2, 538. Also, H. Ewald, Syntax of the Hebrew Language of the Old Testament, 1879 (ET of German 8th edition), prgr. 353 b.

[7] B. S. Childs, A Study of the Formula 'Until this Day,' JBL 82 (1963), 281. Also, Fichtner op. cit. 381. The passages are Gen 26 33b Jos 7 26 Jgs 18 12 II Chr 20 26.

[8] Gen 11 9 21 31 50 11 Ex 15 23 I Chr. 14 11.

[9] Gen 19 22 33 17 II Sam 5 20 Jgs 15 19. Excluded are those passages where the context of Form II is unclear: Gen 25 30b I Chr 11 7b I Sam 23 28 Gen 16 13f. 31 48. Cf. below, 9 f.

[10] Fichtner op. cit. 380.

[11] Ibid. 381.

Only in those few cases in which the phrase modifies the inference
(עַל־כֵּן קָרָא or וַיִּקְרָא in mixed forms) is it related in any direct way
to the nexus of the etiology, namely the causal relation between
event and name (cf. II Chr 20 26 Jos 7 26b Jdc 18 12; also the mixed
form in Jos 5 9). These occurrences may show an original function
for עַד־הַיּוֹם הַזֶּה in the etiological formula[12]. Rather more commonly,
however, the phrase modifies something more distant to the etiology
proper:

    (a) The place which is named
       Mixed Form: Jdc 6 24
       Form II: Jdc 15 19
    (b) The name itself
       Mixed Form: Jdc 1 26
       Form II: Gen 26 33b[13]
    (c) Effect of a story's resolution
       Form I: Gen 19 37. 38

The fundamental agreement in all cases of "until this day" occurring
in the context of Form II or Mixed Form is that the phrase establishes
the extension into the future of something related to the events narrated. But relatively seldom is the nexus of the etiology given a
continuity into the narrator's time[14].

  The task now is to seek the various ways in which these formulae
relate to a narrative context. The focus must be at the earliest visible
stage of tradition history because the attempt is to discover the
characteristics of narrative material which in itself, irrespective of its
final position in a literary complex, functions integrally with the
etymological etiological formula to explain the origin and meaning
of a name. Obviously, therefore, those occurrences of the formulae
which are literary glosses on received tradition as well as those cases
in which the earlier connections in the growth of traditions are quite
obscure, are immediately eliminated from the discussion. The occurrences remaining are then grouped, through literary and tradition
history criticism, according to the degree of complexity of narrative
material surrounding the formula. The examination then proceeds
from simplest to most complex examples and reveals in the progression various, but repetitive, relational lines existing between formula
and its accompanying "story" matter.

---

[12] Childs op. cit. 281 f.

[13] The formula here is defective, since the usual verb, qr', is missing in MT, though
 attested in LXX. It stands closest, however, to Form II.

[14] Childs op. cit. 282. On the Mixed Forms, cf. below, 37 ff.

PART A. ETYMOLOGY OF FORM II TYPE

1. Occurrences eliminated from discussion

a) A literary gloss

Gen 25 30b appears to be a gloss for the following reasons:

(1) The clumsiness of the expression מִן־הָאָדֹם הָאָדֹם הַזֶּה and the sudden shift in vocabulary from נוִד (v. 29. 34) to הָאָדֹם (v. 30).

(2) The connection of Esau with Edom elsewhere is very weak (Gen 32 4 36 1. 8. 19).

(3) The name tradition, especially v. 30b, clearly is a digressive motif, since the whole piece (v. 29-34) focuses on the selling of the birthright[15].

b) Etymological word play missing or obscure

I Chr 11 7b and I Sam 23 28 are grouped here. The former simply reports the designation of a city as "city of David" without the word play characteristic of intentional etymologies (cf. Gen 4 17). This particular half verse may only reflect the Chronicler's penchant for precise identification (cf. I Chr 11 4. 5 5 1ff.).

In the case of I Sam 23 28, the play, if intended, on the name is obscure in the context. The noun מַחְלְקֹת elsewhere appears in a concrete sense as "division" (cf. Jos 11 23 12 7). This meaning can only be applied with difficulty to I Sam 23 28[16]. Others have understood the name as "Rock of Escape(s)." This meaning perhaps fits the context, but is otherwise unattested for חלק[17].

c) Problematical analysis

The classic text difficulties in Gen 16 13f. seriously impair any glimpse of the original connections between v. 14, where Form II occurs, and v. 13 and preceding, where something like Form I appears. The crux of the problem rests in the hopelessly corrupt v. 13b, which since Wellhausen[18] has been emended to read, "Have I really seen God and yet live after seeing him?" This suggestion accords with the sense of the name given in v. 14, and has met with general acceptance. But it, of course, assumes connections which need to be explicit in any study of etiological narrative.

---

[15] Cf. H. Gunkel, Genesis, 1910, 297; E. A. Speiser, Genesis, 1964, 197.

[16] Cf. Driver, Notes on the Hebrew Text . . . of the Books of Samuel, 1913², 190f.

[17] C. H. Gordon, Ugaritic Textbook, 1965, prgr. 19.969 observes that in personnel lists, *ḥlq* appears to be the opposite of "present or accounted for." The texts: 2016: II, 2.4.8.14.18.

[18] Cf. Gunkel, Genesis, 189f., for a summary up to 1910.

In the case of Gen 31 48, a literary analysis of the wider context cannot with any certainty or agreement be carried out. The text suddenly becomes very clumsy in v. 43, and the material which follows seems to reflect a complex intermingling of two accounts of a treaty — perhaps each attached to a different locale. Division of the section into sources is futile, not in the least because the LXX represents still another stage in the complex history of this tradition[19]. Thus a clearly defined narrative context for the etymological formula II in v. 48 cannot be isolated.

2. Simplest report

a) Overview

Three occurrences are grouped in this category: II Chr 20 26 Gen 33 17 (J) Ex 15 23 (J?). All passages reveal Form II at its clearest, and refer to place names. Characteristically, the formula ... עַל־כֵּן קָרָא is the final element in a three part structure:

(1) The locale is mentioned (its name is anticipated)
(2) Report of an event or situation at this location
(3) Inference to the name of the place (Form II)

Each passage expresses a subordinate motif in a larger context.

b) The material

1. II Chr 20 26

There are no sound reasons for considering this verse to be a literary insertion into an older text. Yet there can hardly be any doubt that the etymological motif is subordinate to the narrative movement of the wider context. The main lines move through (1) impending battle (v. 1f.); (2) calling upon Yahweh (v. 3-21); (3) the battle [Yahweh defeats the enemy, spoil is taken, and the troops return home (v. 22-29)]. A parallel sequence appears in II Chr 14 8-14. The broad outline is present also in I Chr 20 1-3 II Chr 25 20-24, and Jos 10 5-15. (More distant, cf. II Chr 34 1-7.) In view of this conventional reporting style, the detail of a name etymology obviously expresses a minor motif. The judgment is further confirmed by the somewhat odd usage of the *kî* subordinating conjunction in v. 26b.

---

[19] Contrast the attempts of J. Wellhausen, Die Composition des Hexateuchs und der Historischen Bücher des Alten Testaments, 1899³, 41f., and Gunkel, Genesis, 350ff., and Speiser, Genesis, 248, and S. R. Driver, The Book of Genesis, 1904², 287. The Greek of v. 46ff. has quite a different sequence of elements.

Its syntactical relation to the immediately preceding clause (v. 26a) is rather loose, but nevertheless typical of II Chronicles. The word introduces material which one would describe in English as parenthetical in relation to its wider context. (Cf. II Chr 7 7 11 21 12 13 28 21, possibly 29 36. Contrast the much more integrative function of causal *kî* in II Chr 20 27.) Thus from the syntactical point of view as well, the name tradition is a subordinate motif. Finally, v. 26 must be viewed as a complete unit here because of the definite shifts in locale which delineate the changing scenes in the whole narrative. The action moves from a vague "wilderness of Tekoa" (v. 20. 24) to "Beracah" (v. 26) to "Jerusalem" (v. 27ff.).

Now v. 26 makes up a simplest Form II report which falls into three distinct parts:

(a) Report of arrival at a particular locale (the name is anticipated)
(b) Report of an event (*kî* clause)
(c) Name tradition (Form II)

The typical features of Form II stand out clearly. The first two elements of the report are most naturally understood as historical narration employing Qatal verb forms as English preterite. They report actions successive in time. But with the final element, the narrative movement ceases, and a conclusion is drawn. Here a definite logical transition from event (act of "blessing") to a name (Valley of Blessing) is made. The relation between the two elements is defined by the assonantal word play. Moreover, the subject of the verb קראו must be indefinite, as the act of calling is given a continuity in time by the addition of עד־היום[20].

2. Gen 33 17 (J)

This verse presents a picture similar to the above. Although the verse is not totally independent of the preceding account (v. 1-11. 12-16) concerning Jacob and Esau, it surely is subordinate to the main dramatic development. Indeed, v. 17 is perhaps best seen as one of a series of loosely linked reports (v. 18. 19f.) which follow the connected narrative[21].

---

[20] The Chronicler is accustomed to using third masculine plural for an indefinite construction. Cf. II Chr 16 14 25 28 27 9 I Chr 24 4. So A. Kropat, Die Syntax des Autors der Chronik, 1909, 7.

[21] For example, cf. G. von Rad, Genesis (ET of German edition of 1956), 323; Gunkel, Genesis, 368. M. Noth speaks of a "short etiological note." (Überlieferungsgeschichte des Pentateuch, 1948, 111.)

As a complete unit, the verse comprises a simplest Form II report in which the locale to be named is specified, event(s) reported,
and a name deduced. The inferential movement typically is shown
by עַל־כֵּן and the logical link made with the use of סכת in both
report and name. The sharpness of the distinction between inferential
and narrative function is somewhat diminished by the ambiguity in
the subject of קרא. Does one translate "Therefore he (Jacob) called
the name of the place Succoth," or "Therefore (that is why) one calls
the place Succoth"? In view of the discussion above (p. 7), the
latter choice seems more likely. In any case, the inferential function
is clear, and contrasts with the simple historical recitation in the
preceding material (ויבן and נסע and עשה).

3. Ex 15 23

This verse likely preserves another example of the simplest
Form II report. The verse appears in the midst of an old tradition
(v. 22b-25a) now framed by P itinerary notes (v. 22a. 27) and expanded
by a piece probably stemming from the Dtr school (v. 25b-26)[22]. Noth[23]
has argued that the "murmuring" motif (v. 24) is relatively young
since the facts given presuppose at most only that the people be
threatened by a lack of food or water. The earliest form of the tradition, then, may have involved only v. 22b-23. 25a. But this is not
sure. In any case, the etymological motif is now subordinate to the
thematic lines which reach their climax in the granting of palatable
water (v. 25a)[24].

Only to this extent is one justified in observing that v. 23, when
viewed alone, comprises a typical Form II simplest report. There is
a locale mentioned, anticipating the name, the report of a situation
and its cause, and an inference to a name — cast in clear impersonal
terms since the singular subject of qr' has no referent, and contrasting with the historical narrative tenses all around (לא יכלו לשתה ;ויבאו;
v. 24 וילנו; v. 25 ויצעק). This simplest report, however, is now
integrally woven into the fabric of the larger "wonder" legend in
such a way that the grounds for the name's derivation are also the
presupposition for the story's resolution. There is no question, then,
of the whole functioning to explain the name in v. 23.

---

[22] M. Noth, Exodus (ET of German edition of 1959), 127; G. Beer, Exodus, 1939, 85,
differs only slightly.

[23] Noth, Pentateuch, 135.

[24] H. Gressmann, Die Anfänge Israels, 1914, 77, and B. Baentsch, Exodus, Leviticus,
Numeri, 1903, 142, and others, reading ממרה in v. 23 as "because of bitterness,"
take כי מרים הם as an explanatory gloss. Later critics generally do not follow
this suggestion.

3. *Simple report*

a) Overview

Four occurrences of Form II are described here as simple report: Gen 50 11 I Chr 14 11 // II Sam 5 20, and Jdc 18 12. They all have to do with place names and express a subordinate motif in a wider context. In all four passages, the basic features of the simplest Form II report are present and surpassed. New material generally described as a narrative setting has been introduced and related organically, but in various ways, to the etiological inference. Each report expresses a subordinate motif in a larger whole. Only one, Gen 50 10b-11, gives evidence of being a secondary *literary* expansion.

1. Gen 50 11

In general, v. 1-14 of chapter 50 have been identified essentially as J material with fragments of E (chiefly in v. 9-10a) and P (v. 12-13)[25]. Noth has proposed alternatively to view v. 1-10a. 14a as J and v. 10b-11 as an expansion by a JE redactor, but using E material[26]. In favor of this general division is the fact that v. 9, usually cited as E, is not really parallel to v. 7. 8 of J. Furthermore, v. 9 continues the image of large numbers so prominent in v. 7b-8. But with v. 10b begins a real doublet: the mourning over Jacob's body is reported a second time. The verse suddenly introduces a word for "mourning" (אבל) which contrasts with v. 10a (ויספדו מספד), and which is clearly linked to the paronomasia on the place name in v. 11. Moreover, in v. 10b a singular verb appears rather abruptly. In view of all this, it seems reasonable to consider v. 10b-11 as a secondary expansion on older tradition.

Now the unit v. 10b-11 falls into three main divisions:

(1) Setting (report of mourning v. 10b)
(2) Action
    (a) Witnessing the mourning (locale specified)
    (b) Speech of the witnesses
(3) Inference to a name (geographical note)

The features characteristic of the Form II simplest report are present here: locale (although the name is not anticipated), reported event(s), inference to the name (formulated with על-כן and an impersonal subject since the singular has no clear referent)[27].

---

[25] Cf. Gunkel, Genesis, 487ff., and Speiser, Genesis, 373ff. Most recently and thoroughly, L. Ruppert, Die Josephserzählung der Genesis, 1965, 190ff.

[26] Noth, Pentateuch, 37f. and 31. Verses 12f. stem from P.

[27] Even though grammatically possible, the subject is hardly "Joseph."

What is new here is the expanded report structure which functions integrally to provide the basis for the inference. A setting given in v. 10b reports the general situation, but already anticipates what is to follow by sounding the catch word (אבל) and by providing the condition upon which the successive events arise. These in turn, specifically the Canaanites' speech, furnish the direct foundation for the inference to the name. In light of the narrative structure, the cessation of narrative movement in the conclusive clause (על־כן ... קרא) is even more striking. The expression contrasts with the preceding succession of *waw* conversive Yiqtal forms (ויעש; ויאמר; וירא) and their resumption in v. 12. Yet the whole piece is held together by the repetition of the key word אבל. There is no doubt that v. 10b-11 function as a unit to explain a name[28].

2. I Chr 14 11 (= II Sam 5 20)

There is no reason to consider v. 11 a secondary insertion into the Chronicles text[29]. But the etymological tradition clearly plays a subordinate role in the wider thematic development. The reported events move through a conventional sequence:

(1) Threat to the people — v. 9
(2) Consultation with Yahweh. Divine answer
(3) Action on the basis of answer — v. 11 (removal of the threat, i. e. defeat of the enemy)

One sees, of course, this structure in the parallel passage II Sam 5 17-21. It is also obvious in I Chr 14 13-16 (= II Sam 5 22-25), I Sam 23 1-5 (expanded with the motif of fearful inaction), and less clearly in Jdc 20 18-35 and I Sam 30 7ff.[30]. The whole narrative can be rounded off with a concluding summary statement (I Chr 14 17 I Sam 23 5 Jdc 20 36). Although the name tradition in I Chr 14 11 is inseparable from this structural context, it is clearly a minor motif outside the main thematic lines. It is related to them only as a consequence of the conventional conclusion to the narrative, i. e., the victory over the threatening armies. The etymology itself is based only on material given in v. 11. If these judgments are correct, one can view the name

---

[28] A similar pun on a place name may be extant in Ugaritic in 3 Aqht : 8 which reads:
. . . *qrt ablm*
ablm (qrt zbl yrḫ)
". . . city of mourners, Ablm city of prince YRḪ."

[29] Cf. Rothstein and Hänel, Das erste Buch der Chronik, 1927, vol. I 264f. Also E. L. Curtis, A Critical and Exegetical Commentary of the Books of Chronicles, 1910, 208f.

[30] Cf. further von Rad, Der Heilige Krieg im Alten Israel, 1951, 6ff.

tradition, which on account of the stereotype Form II structure must encompass all of v. 11, as a distinctive building block supplementing the larger conventional narrative sequence.

The characteristics of Form II simplest report appear in v. 11. The locale is identified, anticipating the name[31]; events are reported (victory and a speech on that occasion), and the inference to the name made. The conclusive clause is impersonally formulated, since the Chronicler frequently employs the third masculine plural verb in this way[32], and since the plural has no clear reference to a definite antecedent. The causal link between event (speech) and name is clear in the double assonance.

The material however shows its greater complexity in its highly integrated structure. The basis for the name does not lie in a mere report of an event. Rather the name is derived from a speech which must be understood as a response to the previously reported victory. In short, the situation in which the name might arise (victory) also motivates the speech and therefore is a presupposition for understanding the inference to the name. The series of *waw* conversive Yiqtal verb forms also in this case shows the unity of the whole piece. The contrast, moreover, between this narrative style and the etymological formula sharply defines the latter's inferential function in the midst of recitation.

The analysis and conclusions for the parallel account in II Sam 5 20 do not differ substantially. One need only note that the translation of the formula here is less surely to be made with an indefinite subject. The Greek MSS are uniform in reading for MT על־כן קרא, aorist passive δια τουτο εκληθη. But this in itself is of little help, since the LXX consistently reads in II Sam the aorist passive for every etymology regardless of whether MT has על־כן קרא(ו) or ויקרא את־שם or Niph קרא (2 16 5 9 5 20 6 8. The only exception is 12 28). The most that can be claimed is that the inferential function of Form II is somewhat blurred by the ambiguity in the grammar. Yet the formal aspects of this passage follow so closely the usual pattern that one should not see a basic alteration in the etymological form.

3. Jdc 18 12

Since the period of Wellhausen[33], the dominant literary critical approach to Jdc 17—18 has been to see here a narrative composed

---

[31] Probably read with two MSS, LXX, and Syriac the singular ויעל for MT ויעלו. The edition of the LXX used: A Brooke, McLean, and Thackeray, ed., The Old Testament in Greek, 1932.

[32] Kropat, Syntax, 7.

[33] Composition 227f. He saw one basic stratum with all sorts of interpolations.

of two sources, whether J or E or simply "older" and "younger"[34].
The question is still debatable, and more recently the one-source-
plus-expansions theory has been revived again with force[35]. In any
case, both from a literary critical and history of traditions point of
view, the etiological etymological material in 18 11f. appears at best
as a minor element in the wider context. The location which receives
a name in fact is only an interim stopping place on the way to the
main conquest (18 27ff.; cf. v. 13). Moreover, the explanation of the
name requires nothing more than is given in v. 11f.[36].

Verse 12 alone exhibits the characteristic features of the simplest
Form II report. An event is reported, along with its location (v. 12a)
and the inference (formulated with indefinite subject) is drawn[37].
Typically, the assonance between the name and the verb used in the
reported event makes clear the logical link between narration (note
coordinate style ויעלו and ויחנו) and inference.

Yet the sense of the name is not given completely in v. 12. The
setting reported in v. 11, with its image of a large group arrayed for
war, and the identification of this company with the Danites, is
organically related to v. 12. The descriptive vocabulary is commensurate with both the motif of "camping" and the military flavor of
מחנה in the name[38]. Moreover, the connection of the place with the
Danites, as reflected in the name itself and crucial to its explanation,
is made explicit only insofar as v. 11 functions to identify the agents
for the ensuing action.

Thus the whole piece is built integrally as a simple report. To
the basic structure of Form II has been added a rather detailed setting which provides information necessary to the sense of the inferred name. Obviously in this case the basis for the inference does not
rest in merely one element of the report. Rather, the narrator draws
a conclusion which is indicated by the action reported as well as
information supplied by the descriptive setting.

---

[34] Cf. such commentaries as G. Moore, A Critical and Exegetical Commentary on the
Book of Judges, 1895; K. Budde, Das Buch der Richter, 1897; D. W. Nowack,
Richter, Ruth und Bücher Samuelis, 1902; O. Eissfeldt, Die Quellen des Richter-
buches, 1925; C. A. Simpson, Composition of the Book of Judges, 1957.

[35] H. W. Hertzberg, Die Bücher Josua, Richter, Ruth, 1953, 237 ff. Cf. now M. Noth,
The Background of Jdc. 17—18, in: Israel's Prophetic Heritage, Essays in honor
of James Muilenburg, ed. B. Anderson, 1962, 68 ff.

[36] Literary critics agree in keeping v. 11f. essentially in one stratum. Cf. the commentaries. Noth, Pentateuch, 70, speaks of an "etiological note."

[37] The phrase הנה אחרי קרית יערים is likely a gloss, since it differs slightly from
the location given in v. 12a.

[38] Cf. Ex 14 19f. 24 Jos 6 11. 14. 28 10 5f. 15 11 4 (cf. 11 5) Jdc 7 9ff. et al.

4. Developed report and/or scene

a) Overview

The occurrences of Form II grouped here have to do with names of places (Gen 19 22 21 31) and a spring (Jdc 15 19). These formulae differ from each other only insofar as their respective context includes conversation. But they all occur as a part of a narrative structure which shows clearly a dramatic movement from problem to solution (Jdc 15 18f. Gen 19 17-22) or analogously, proposal to agreed action (Gen 21 22ff.). Yet for all this thematic development, the essential inferential characteristics of simplest and simple Form II reports are preserved. All passages except Gen 19 17-22 reflect an origin independent of their immediate contexts. It is not a question of merely subordinate motifs in a larger whole, but rather one of independent reports or scenes arising on the oral level quite separately from their present literary context.

b) The material

1. Jdc 15 19

There is little doubt that v. 18f. preserve a local tradition whose origin was independent of the account of Samson's victory over the Philistines. The piece is complete in itself, adds nothing to the preceding narrative, and in no way depends upon it for its meaning[39]. Moreover, הערלים as a title is used only here in Judges, contrasting sharply with 15 1-17. 20. Probably v. 18f. were related to the victory story because both blocks narrated events set at Lehi. Verse 20 stems from the Dtr redaction[40].

The essential structural features of Form II are present in this unit. Events are reported as occurring at a particular locale. Though the name of the spring is not anticipated in v. 19a, the phraseology (*the* hollow place at Lehi) leaves little doubt that the spot was definite and well known[41]. An inference to a name (not clearly formulated with an indefinite subject)[42] is then drawn on the basis of reported action. The logical link is accomplished through assonance (ויקרא v. 18 and הקורא v. 19b).

---

[39] Cf. Gressmann, Anfänge, 254; Nowack, Richter, 130ff.; Simpson, Composition, 60; Hertzberg, Josua, Richter, 231.

[40] Cf. the commentaries. Also cf. M. Noth, Überlieferungsgeschichtliche Studien, 1943, 61, and more recently, W. Richter, Die Bearbeitungen des "Retterbuches" in der deuteronomischen Epoche, 1964, 75.

[41] The word בלחי in v. 19a has been interpreted as "in the jawbone," rather than the place name, "in Lehi." This does not seem likely, particularly in view of the etymological pattern which nearly always mentions a locale for the reported events.

[42] The Greek MSS, however, read aorist passive: διὰ τοῦτο ἐκλήθη.

In terms of narrative structure, what is new is that the report moves through a dramatic sequence. The problem simply and abruptly stated in v. 18 "and he was very thirsty," is finally resolved when God brings forth water in v. 19a and Samson is revived. The transition between problem and its solution is made with the pleas reported in v. 18b. Hence these two verses are structured according to a design which moves toward a well defined goal; they merit a label of "developed report."

It is important to note that the inference to the name is based upon a crucial element in the thematic development. Yet the essential logical relationships found in the least complex examples of Form II are undisturbed here by the more expansive details provided in the movement from problem to solution. This fact is important in understanding the limitations imposed upon free creativity by the tenacity of a fixed etymological form.

2. Gen 21 31

The text in Gen 21 22-34 reflects in its disunity and irregularities a complex history of transmission. A covenant is reported twice (v. 27b. 32a); two gifts are presented to Abimelek (v. 27a. 28-30); two different puns on the place name seem to have been interwoven: שבע = "seven" (v. 28. 29. 30) and שבע = "oath" or "swear" (v. 23. 24. 31). Moreover, v. 33f. are thematically quite unrelated to all this. Verse 34 particularly gives every appearance of stemming from a redactor.

In general, there are two distinctive thematic groupings of material. One speaks of a disagreement over water rights. Abraham initiates the action which leads to his presenting a gift to Abimelek as attestation of his rightful ownership of the disputed well (v. 25f. 28-30). The second grouping centers on a concordat. Here Abimelek, not Abraham, initiates the action by calling for a kind of non-aggression pact, an "oath" (v. 22-24). Presumably the conclusion to this affair is given in v. 27 and 31, since the former cannot belong with the water strife tradition, and the latter is linked explicitly to the oath theme[43].

Now the "oath-covenant" traditions (Block A = v. 22-24. 27. 31) most likely were preserved in the E document, since אלהים appears consistently here. But it is still debatable whether or not the other grouping (B Block = v. 25-26. 28-30) should be assigned to J[44]. It is

---

[43] Cf. von Rad, Genesis, 230 ff.

[44] Cf. for example, Gunkel, Genesis, 233 f., who speaks of E with a J variant. Skinner, A Critical and Exegetical Commentary on Genesis, 1910, 214 ff., and Speiser, Genesis, 159 f., attempted to read the account as a unified composition. This is impossible

possible, of course, that B is merely a variant, or perhaps just an expansion with an etymological interest on the primary "concordat" tradition. If both circles contain an important interest in explaining the name Beersheba, it is odd that only one stylized etymological formula is preserved, and this indissolubly linked with the A material (v. 31)[45]. Such a situation is best explained if the B tradition is an expansion on an already fixed concordat account. Moreover, the parallel tradition which connects the events with Isaac (Gen 26 26ff.) is the older, according to Noth[46]. Yet the material there knows nothing of a disputed well at Beersheba. Thus the question is at least open whether or not the B grouping in Gen 21 is a secondary elaboration on the A tradition.

In any case, it seems reasonably certain on both literary and tradition history grounds that v. 22-24. 27. 31 may be studied as an independent account. As such, the unit is a dramatic scene (there is conversation) consisting of four major divisions:

(1) Proposal for an oath: v. 22f.
(2) Response: v. 24
(3) Report of covenant made: v. 27
(4) Inference to a name: v. 31 (Form II)

The typical characteristics of Form II are visible here. An inference to a name is formulated with an indefinite subject[47] and contrasts with the historical narrative movement preceding. The assonance between the name and the use of נשבע in the reported conversation (v. 22b-24) makes clear the basis for the logical inference.

The scene is certainly a tightly knit and rounded off piece. The beginning is typically constructed (ויהי בעת ההוא cf. Gen 26 32 38 1 I Reg 11 29 et al.). It quickly provides a setting and a proposal to be acted upon. The movement from proposition to action, analogous to the way from problem to solution, constitutes the narrative. Yet the sparseness of actual third person narration in relation to the quoted conversation indicates that the emphasis rests upon the latter.

---

and leads the interpreter to supply speculative connections between the two traditions.

[45] The *kî* clause in v. 31b undoubtedly links the whole verse with the "oath" motif. The judgment that in the history of this Form II, such explanatory clauses represent a secondary development, does not lead necessarily to the conclusion that a *literary* gloss has made the connection with the "oath" motif in this case. Indeed, the text gives no indication of literary disturbance at this point.

[46] Noth, Pentateuch, 141 ff.

[47] The use of third plural with definite subjects in v. 27 and 31b makes it likely that the subject of singular *qr'* is indefinite rather than specifically Abimelek or Abraham. However, the LXX reads aorist.

It is not surprising, therefore, that the word plays, and hence the
basis for the inference, appear conspicuously at this point. There can
be little doubt that the etymology is integrally connected with the
scene preceding.

One must reckon, however, with certain atypical features of this
material. In the first place, the locale for the action is nowhere specified in the narrative preceding the name formula. This may be an
unimportant omission. It may, however, indicate a shift from the
clearest examples of a Form II report and a step toward mixing with
the pattern of Form I. The omission raises at the same time another
interesting question. The usual way of picturing etiological creativity
is to see it as a speculative movement from a known (effect) to an
unknown (cause)[48]. If this be correct, then the absence of a specified
location for the reported events may indicate that this movement
from known to unknown has begun to break down and an increased
interest in simple narration without etiological impetus is emerging.

Secondly, Form II appears here in an expanded form. A clause
subordinated to the main conclusive formula by means of causal *kî*
explicitly reports a basis for the inference to the name. The word
play already noted between v. 23f. and the name is picked up with
reference this time to an action only implied in the prior narration
(v. 24. 27). The addition of the *kî* clause is surely secondary in the
history of Form II[49]. (It is missing also in the older account in Gen
26 33.) But if its appearance here is due to the influence of the established pattern of Form I, as Fichtner judges, then again one suspects
that a mixed form is beginning to emerge.

These atypical features are important in showing the fluidity of
the etymological material. In my opinion, they do not override the
essential inferential relationship between narration and name. Thus
one is justified in viewing Gen 21 22-24. 27. 31 as a scene showing clear
dramatic development, organically related to a Form II etymological
conclusion, and functioning to provide the reason for a particular
name[50].

3. Gen 19 17-22 (23)

These verses are generally viewed by commentators as secondary
intrusions into an older account of the destruction of Sodom and

---

[48] Cf. C. Westermann, Arten der Erzählung in der Genesis, in: Forschung am Alten
Testament, 1964, 43. Also M. P. Nilsson, Geschichte der griechischen Religion,
vol. I/2, 25ff. L. Röhrich, Märchen und Wirklichkeit, 1964², 27—36. Cf. above, iff.

[49] Cf. above, 6ff. and Fichtner op. cit. 380.

[50] The parallel account in Gen 26 23-33 is discussed below as a fully developed narrative
involving more than one scene.

Gomorrah[51]. They break the continuity between v. 16 and 24, contradict somewhat the sense and mood of the resolution point reached in v. 16, and show a certain disturbance in the confusion over whether one (v. 18b. 19-22) or more (v. 17a. 18a) agents are speaking with Lot. Contrast v. 19, which consistently uses singular address, with v. 2 where Lot speaks in precisely parallel expression and uses plural forms consistent with the number of addressees. (Cf. v. 7. 8.) Moreover, the etymological motif here is distinctly subordinate to the main thematic lines of 19 1-28[52].

As separate tradition, then, v. 17-23 comprise a narrative scene with clear Form II characteristics. An inference to a name comes in v. 22b. It is likely formulated with an indefinite subject, although certainty on this point is not forthcoming. In any case, עַל־כֵּן makes the inferential function clear, if not absolutely free of narrative force. The contrast is apparent with the narrative tenses preceding the formula (וַיֹּאמֶר in v. 17. 18. 21). The logical movement is typically expressed in the assonance between words in Lot's speech (v. 20) and the name (v. 22b). The absence of a specific mention of a locale here may not be important, since the inference does not rest upon an event at the place so named.

The passage is a tightly constructed unity. While it is not quite appropriate to speak of a dramatic tension reaching resolution (since the piece is nearly all conversation), there is a certain thematic movement from a command given along with a threatened disaster to a final stay in the execution of punishment along with a new command. Within this structure, the name is clearly inferred from a key element, i. e., Lot's plea (v. 20). There is little doubt, then, that the whole scene functions as a unit to provide an explanatory base for the name.

5. Narrative

a) Overview

The two passages classified here (Gen 26 23-33 11 1-9) bring a Form II etymological formula into organic relation to a narrative context consisting of at least two dramatic scenes. Otherwise, they show the essential pattern already discovered in less complex materials, and clearly function — in all their artistic development — to provide a basis for a particular name. Each narrative or story, al-

---

[51] Cf. Gunkel, Genesis, 206; Procksch, Die Genesis, 1924, 129; C. A. Simpson, The Early Traditions of Israel, 1948, 78; Skinner, Genesis, 309.

[52] Cf. von Rad, Genesis, 215.

though now in the J document, originated independently and dealt
with a place name.

b) The material

1. Gen 26 33 (J)

The pericope spanning v. 23-33, while linked in the redaction to
the preceding reports of well diggings (v. 17ff.), resists full assimila-
tion to its literary position. The location changes (v. 23), and the
absence of a dispute motif separates it clearly in the history of traditions from the block in v. 17-22. Surely v. 34 is unrelated to this
Beersheba tradition. Moreover, the covenant theme of v. 26ff. does not
quite harmonize with the parting implied in v. 16. Thus to all appearances, the Beersheba account originated quite independently of these
surrounding Isaac traditions[53].

Within the pericope, v. 24-25a (theophany and altar building) are
generally recognized as a later stage in the traditional development[54].
It is to be argued below that v. 32-33a resulted from secondary expansion on the name etiology[55]. Thus the earliest visible stage of the
tradition included v. 25b-31. 33b[56]. This complex, similar to the variant in Gen 21, falls roughly into four main divisions:

Scene I
    (1) Proposal for action: v. 28
    (2) Response: (report of feasting)
Scene II
    (1) Action carried out: (report of oath made)
    (2) Inference to a name

Characteristically for Form II, the narrative movement ceases
with עַל־כֵּן and an inference is drawn to a name. This inferential
function is not at all impeded by the absence of קָרָא[57]. The nominal
phrase plus its adverbial modifier "as at this day" is best read in the
general present. Consequently, its force as a logical conclusion is
strengthened, and the contrast with the preceding coordinate recita-
tion, sharpened (v. 28 וַיֹּאמֶר v. 30 וַיַּעַשׂ; וַיֹּאכְלוּ; וַיִּשְׁתּוּ). The inference,

---

[53] Ibid. 264ff. Cf. also Noth, Pentateuch, 114—118. 170f.

[54] Gunkel, Genesis, 303; Noth, Pentateuch, 30. But cf. Skinner, Genesis, 366.

[55] Cf. below 34ff.

[56] Verse 23 functions as a transitional piece and thus may stem from the redactor
(cf. v. 17). Yet a location is normally given in the old altar-building report schema
(cf. Gen 12 7 13 14ff. 35 6). On the other hand, a locale is usually given with
Form II etymologies. Thus one cannot surely judge in which layer v. 23 originally
belonged.

[57] LXX[A] has εκαλεσεν.

as the assonance indicates, is based directly upon the action reported in v. 31 (וישבעו), and no doubt indirectly upon the complex of ideas associated with covenant making[58]. Hence a conclusion is drawn from a reported event (v. 31) and from the substance of the whole piece.

Form II is part of a tightly structured whole. In two scenes, each marked by the passage of time, the dramatic movement from proposal to action is completed. Narrative details which do not seem essential to this thematic development (e. g., v. 26f. and 30) are clearly not on that account extraneous. Verses 26f. not only provide a setting for the events to follow, but make an important connection to 26 16. And v. 30, of course, records a typical feature of covenant ceremonies, i. e., the meal (cf. Gen 31 54 Ex 24 11). Most important, however, is the fact that the basis for the inference lies in a key element in the dramatic development. It is the very fulfillment of the opening proposal which leads logically to the particular place name. Clearly, therefore, the whole narrative functions as a unit to ground the name Beersheba.

2. Gen 11 9 (J)

Verses 1-9 clearly form a completed and rounded off narrative. But they have occasioned great debate on the question of source division[59]. Gunkel[60], followed by others[61], saw two parallel recensions, each containing an etiological motif. One told of building a tower in order to make a name (etiology on the city name *Babel*); the other spoke of building a city so as not to be dispersed throughout the earth (etiology on the diverse and scattered populations). What is clear after all is that there is now no satisfactory way to recover consistently these supposed versions. The city motif only with great difficulty can be separated from the tower theme in v. 4f. In the cuneiform traditions which lay in the formative background of the Genesis account[62], tower (sanctuary) is already linked and even blurred with, the city of Babylon[63]. Moreover, v. 8a and 9b form a very awkward, if not improbable, ending to a "city version." The difficulties cannot be solved on the literary level. It seems best to recognize the inconsistencies and diverse themes, and to accept the piece as an essen-

---

[58] Cf. D. J. McCarthy, Three Covenants in Genesis, CBQ 26 (1964), 179 ff.

[59] Cf. the summary in B. S. Childs, A Study of Myth in Genesis (part I of dissertation, Basel, 1955), 94 f.

[60] Genesis 92 ff.

[61] E. g., Procksch, Genesis, 89; Skinner, Genesis, 224.

[62] Gunkel, Genesis, 94. Recently, E. A. Speiser, Word Plays on the Creation Epic's Version of the Founding of Babylon, Orientalia 25 (1956), 21 ff.

[63] Enuma Elish VI, lines 60 ff. 72. Cf. the latest translation in ANET² 68 f.

tially unified product of long development ending with the fixing in
one literary source, J.

In this way, the etymological etiology can be examined with due
regard for the problems and limitations of defining a narrative context organically related to the name formula.

Some characteristic features of Form II are apparent, however.
The על-כן clause clearly draws an inference. The singular subject of
qr' can only refer to Yahweh in this context. But this is a highly
unlikely reading. Therefore, the inference must be understood with
an indefinite subject. Moreover, the על-כן clause marks a cessation
of narrative movement, contrasting sharply with the string of *waw*
conversives (v. 1-8) which recite a series of successive events. The
basis for the inference is made plain by the assonantal word play
between Yahweh speech and name (v. 7 and 9a). Finally, a locale is
mentioned in the opening of the account, albeit rather vaguely specified (v. 2)[64].

Despite the lack of cohesion in the whole narrative, certain general features parallel those found in more clearly defined Form II
passages. There are two distinct scenes, marked by chronological and
thematic shifts (v. 1-4. 5-8). More importantly, a thematic sequence
from proposed to thwarted action reaches its climax in Yahweh's
direct action (v. 8).

But there are features atypical to Form II. First, the inference
to a name is based upon the Yahweh speech presented as a response
to the building activities of man (v. 7). Yet the actual content of the
speech somewhat resists its literary location, for its most direct reference is to the theme of one language (v. 1. 6a) rather than to the
building motif dominant in v. 2-5. Thus it is not quite appropriate to
say that the name of the city is based upon a *key* element in the
preceding narrative. Only insofar as the Yahweh speech now functions structurally as a direct response to the proposed action (v. 3f.)
can one see it as a crucial part of the thematic development. Hence
the problematic nature of the material immediately causes some qual-
ification of the more typical integral relation between narrative and
name.

Secondly, the name formula has been expanded with a *ki* clause
in a way parallel to Gen 21 31[65]. The focus of the word play is shifted,
consequently, to a word descriptive of an act only implied in the
preceding narrative. Thus the logical relationships are somewhat
broadened. The inference draws upon a Yahweh speech as well as
the implicit action following it. As mentioned in connection with

---

[64] The "land of Shinar" designates elsewhere a Babylonian area: Gen 10 10 (J) Dan 1 2.
[65] Cf. above 20.

Gen 21 31, this addition of a *kî* clause may represent early signs of a blurring of the pattern with that of Form I.

Viewed as a whole, it is clear that the force of the Form II structure was a significant factor in the shaping of this material. There is justification, therefore, for understanding its role in grounding a name to be at least equal in importance to other indigenous functions.

6. Appendix

Sufficiently positive evidence for isolating a particular narrative context for Form II is lacking in the case of Jos 7 26. Most critics find an essentially unified block of tradition once the Ai material (v. 2-5a) has been bracketed[66]. There are a few expansions, perhaps. But the dramatic movement from Yahweh's anger (v. 1) to its abating (v. 26a) is quite pronounced, and shows the essential unity of the whole piece.

The question remains, however, whether or not the name etymology is integral to the main traditions[67]. Certainly there are no serious grounds for suspecting a literary insertion here. But the text of v. 26 is disturbing. For one thing, there appear to be preserved two divergent etiological motifs: a pile of stones and a place name. Elsewhere, whenever Form II (or Form I or a mixed form) occurs with the explicit mention of a permanent effect existing "until this day," it is the effect itself which receives a name. (Cf. for example, Jdc 15 19 Jdc 6 24.) Such is not the case in Jos 7 26. Hence these two traditions were likely originally independent of each other, and subsequently fused.

Secondly, the central oracle in v. 13-15 stipulates that the punishment for the violation of the *ḥerem* is to be by fire (v. 15). Yet in the resolution of the account, execution by stoning has almost supplanted the "burning" motif (v. 25). One wonders, therefore, whether the interest in stones might represent a secondary tradition.

Finally, the etymological material in v. 26 actually involves only v. 25 and the formula in v. 26b. At best this can only express a minor

---

[66] C. Steuernagel, Das Deuteronomium und das Buch Josua, 1923², 175ff.; G. Hölscher, Die Anfänge der hebräischen Geschichtsschreibung, 1942, 340; Noth, Das Buch Josua, 1953², 43ff.; Hertzberg, Josua, Richter, 48ff.; H. Holzinger, Das Buch Josua, 1901, 19ff., leaves open the question between a one source with expansions view and a theory of conflated composite accounts. Gressmann, Anfänge, 141ff., defended two parallel accounts here.

[67] Noth (Josua, 43ff.) argues that it is primary. Childs, JBL 82 (1963), 288, affirms exactly the opposite.

theme in the whole. At the least, the situation raises the possibility
that the name etiology is younger than the preceding story.

Obviously the evidence for the primary or secondary character
of this etymological material is inconclusive. However, in terms of
the established Form II patterns, something more can be suggested.
There are some typical features. A locale, anticipating the name, is
specified (v. 24b); a speech is reported which by assonance forms the
basis for an inference (with indefinite subject) to the name. Here,
then, are the essential elements for simplest Form II. But they are
now broken apart by v. 25b-26a. Even assuming that the interest in
the pile of stones is expressed in younger tradition, the simplest
Form II structure is seriously disturbed by the report of burning,
i. e., narrative material which reports the resolution to the tension
raised in v. 1 and 15. Moreover, the etymological elements comprise
neither a simple nor a developed report. Nothing of an integrated
unit, such as was evident in the study of Gen 50 10b-11 or I Chr 14 11,
or a clear dramatic sequence as in Jdc 15 18f., can be made out of
the name tradition alone. At every point one must go outside of
v. 25f. to find structural elements which might provide an organic
context for the etymological features. Just at this point, however,
there are difficulties because the inference to the name is not based
upon a crucial or necessary element in the overall thematic unit.
This essential feature of a genuine etymological narrative is not visible here; the way from tension to resolution can be traversed without Joshua's execution speech in v. 25[68]. Hence, the entire Achan
tradition cannot be said to have originally provided a basis for the
name of the valley, simply because the structural features which
would indicate such a function are absent. One might even suppose
that the etymological elements, given their lack of unity, are later
accretions onto fixed traditions which served some other end[69].

7. Summary and conclusions

The simplest occurrence of Form II reveals a fixed structure:
(1) Reported event
(2) Inference to a name based upon this report

---

[68] The issue is not whether v. 25 is secondary to its context, but whether it is subordinate. Regardless of how one decides this question, it is clear that the speech
is not a crucial step in moving from tension to resolution. Compare for example,
the importance of Achan's confession (v. 20) to the thematic development.

[69] The fact that the Greek (and parallels elsewhere) reads *Achar* for MT *Achan* does
not argue necessarily for the originality of the etymological interest. It may indicate
further development in the direction of more word play.

Often, narrative material anticipates the name, and nearly always gives a specific location for the event. This functional connection between narration and name is constitutive. It remains essentially unaltered in a full range of complexity — from simplest report to genuine narrative.

The scope of narrative material which shows this organic link with an etymological formula is very limited. Never is Form II the focus of extensive traditions. The two most complex cases (Gen 11 1-9 and 26 23-33) scarcely cover more than 10 verses. For the most part, the Old Testament texts preserve short reports which are clearly secondary, or at least subordinate, to a larger narrative complex.

PART B. ETYMOLOGY OF FORM I TYPE

1. Cases eliminated from the discussion

a) A literary gloss in the text

Clearly Gen 31 47[70] and Ex 18 3[71] fall into this category. Matters are a bit more complex in Jdc 6 32. The etymological formula tends in quite a new direction. Verse 31, with the catchword *rib* used three times, portrays a challenge by Joash that Baal contend *for himself*. The result is never given. But v. 32 presupposes that Baal has responded and contended *against Gideon*. Hence, v. 32 cannot have been the original continuation of v. 31. It is most likely a literary gloss since it is only very loosely related to the story preceding. If so, the oddly suspended clause in v. 31, "for he broke down his altar," having no direct reference to its immediate context, is understandable as a bridge to the etiology on Jerubbaal[72].

b) The etymological interest is missing or obscure

This is the case in I Reg 9 13 II Reg 14 7 Gen 35 15 Gen 35 18[73] and Jdc 1 17[74].

[70] Cf. Gunkel, Genesis, 351 et al.

[71] If not a literary addition to the text, the γ elements of Form I (β is missing) are at least parenthetical and therefore only loosely set into the context. In any case, the formula is broken here. Gen 27 36 probably should be seen as a broken form illustrating more than anything else a delight in word plays.

[72] So, W. Richter, Traditionsgeschichtliche Untersuchungen zum Richterbuch, 1963, 161f. "At that time" may be the work of the redactor also.

[73] Cf. the commentaries for various attempts at reconstructing the significance of these names.

[74] The narrative elements present in a parallel passage, Num 21 1-3, have been covered in Jdc 1 17 by the historian's style of report. A remnant of an etymological etio-

c) Problematic analysis

Five cases are included here: Gen 21 3 Gen 22 14 Gen 32 31 Gen 35 7 Ex 17 7.

1. Gen 21 3

Although Gen 21 1-7 presents difficult problems for literary analysis, it seems most likely that a simplest report, with birth schema, lies in the background of a very complex and well sifted bit of tradition. A satisfactory division into sources has proved to be impossible[75], not the least because of a baffling and inconsistent variation of divine names in the LXX[76]. Clearly, v. 4f. stem from P (cf. Gen 17 9-14). Probably v. 3 is from the priestly source because of the precision with which it is formulated. But the doublets in v. 1a//1b and 6//7 cannot be surely distributed among the literary documents. Although v. 6 and 7 appear to report two different motivations for the name Isaac, this fact alone may only suggest traditional piling up of etymological word plays, perhaps in light of the material found in 18 12. In any case, the verses less the P strains present a fragmentary birth report with an etymological etiology, but this only as a composite literary piece comprising v. 1. 2. 6f. which no longer has preserved a simple report of birth. A smooth, early stage of tradition is not forthcoming.

2. Gen 22 14

As the text in this passage is now vocalized, an allusion is probably made to v. 8 where a similar expression appears. But the relative clause of v. 14 has quite another tendency. Not only does the vocalization יֵרָאֶה obscure any allusion to v. 8, but the formulation of the clause is suited to a proverbial saying (יֵאָמֵר cf. Gen 10 9 Num 21 14) rather than a place name as expected from v. 14a, the typical β element of Form I. Therefore v. 14b cannot be the original γ element

---

logical formula probably remains in the word play. Yet the report of the city name now appears as a digression (cf. v. 20. 21. 23. 26). To all appearances, any interest in explaining the name has receded in favor of making the overall reporting accurately reflect any *changes* in names (cf. v. 10. 11. 23 et al.).

[75] Cf. Gunkel's attempt, Genesis, 226f. and 272, and various disagreements among subsequent commentators. Procksch, Genesis, 137ff.; Driver, Genesis, 209f.; Speiser, Genesis, 153f.

[76] V. 2 κυριος for MT אלהים, but in v. 4 Θεος for MT אלהים. Yet v. 6, Κυριος again for MT אלהים. The use of Κυριος for אלהים is, of course, not unknown elsewhere. Cf. Theological Dictionary of the New Testament, ed. G. Kittel, vol. III, 1059. Yet fluctuations in a rather limited bit of tradition may point to a complex history of the Hebrew text more than to translation idiosyncrasies in the Greek.

belonging with v. 14a; the form has been broken. Moreover, a genuine place name may not even survive here. יהוה יראה looks like an explanation for a now lost name[77].

3. Gen 32 31

In the case of Gen 32 31, Elliger[78] has convincingly argued that a thorough source analysis for Gen 32 23ff. is impossible. Behind the J document lies an obscure and complicated history of oral transmission which is now reflected in the roughness of the narration. The etymological formula strangely floats in its context; its γ element seems appropriate to a theophany (cf. Gen 16 13 Jdc 6 22) while the narrative material of the context does not clearly relate such. Thus a reasonably well defined narrative context for Form I is not forthcoming. Verse 31 may even be a secondary addition to the literary form of the pericope.

4. Gen 35 7

Gen 35 1-7 (verse 7 has Form I) gives every appearance of having been secondarily linked up with the circle of Jacob stories. Alt clearly delineated the character of an older layer of pilgrimage tradition in which Shechem and Bethel were bound together (v. 1-4)[79]. If one must understand the present form of the text as the fulfillment of the vow uttered in 28 20ff., one must see also that the connections are implicit rather than explicit (v. 1. 3). And there is no mention of the tithe of 28 22. Moreover the verses 1-7, especially v. 5ff., lack the cohesion necessary in an originally connected narrative. Verse 5, for example, appears to link the material to the Dinah traditions of chapter 34, but is unrelated to v. 1-4 (the third plural subject of רדפו has no clear reference) or to v. 6ff.[80]. Accordingly, the motivation given for the name in v. 7 is not related to anything reported in the immediately preceding verses. Rather, it is secondary and stems from the redactional linkage made with the Jacob stories[81].

5. Ex 17 7

About all that can be decided by literary criticism in this block (v. 1-7) is that 1bβ-2 // v. 3, and that v. 1a-1bα stem from the P redac-

---

[77] Gunkel, Genesis, 239, in fact reconstructs the lost place name.

[78] Der Jakobskampf am Jabbok, ZthK 48 (1951), 1—31.

[79] Cf. A. Alt, Die Wallfahrt von Sichem nach Bethel in Kleine Schriften, vol. I 1953, 79ff.

[80] Cf. Gunkel, Genesis, 378f. He also characterizes the whole as "redactional work," a "loosely piled heap."

[81] Cf. Noth, Pentateuch, 87; von Rad, Genesis, 331ff.

tor[82]. Some critics have joined v. 7 with 1bβ-2 because of the common occurrence of *rîb*. Yet the whole לאמר clause of v. 7 has no clear reference to the narrative material. At best, a fragment containing a name tradition remains (v. 1bβ-2. 7?). Certainly this is not enough to justify any conclusions[83].

2. Form I report

a) Overview

The very simplest examples of etymological report, of course, are those in which the full Form I is disassociated from any kind of narrative setting. Two passages fit this category: Gen 3 20 and I Chr 4 9[84].

The other occurrences of clear Form I show only a minimal narrative context. They appear in J, E, or JE layers of Genesis, and mostly report the naming of a child at birth. The formula in such cases occurs as a part of a narrative schema which itself can assume, in general, three forms[85]:

A. Narrative: birth (and conception often) reported
   Form I (naming and explanation)
B. Narrative: birth (and conception often) reported
   Note on peculiar characteristics or circumstances
   Form I (naming)
C. Narrative: birth (and often conception) reported
   Saying (usually of the mother)
   Form I (naming; no γ element)

A large number of examples are found in one block of tradition: Gen 29 32. 33 Gen 30 8. 11. 13. 18. 20. 24[86]. Elsewhere: Gen 4 25 5 29

---

[82] Cf. the major commentaries, especially Noth, Exodus, 138 ff.

[83] Noth (Pentateuch, 135 n. 348) is unsure whether or not the name etymology belongs to the oldest layer of the tradition.

[84] There are two cases in which a name etymology is given as a part of a birth prediction (Gen 16 11 and I Chr 22 9). To this group must be added Gen 17 5 which has the Niphal of *qr'*. These passages have in common the fact that something like Form I appears in a speech delivered in the imperative mode. The particular name is grounded only in the *kî* explanatory clause (Gen 16 11) or a feature in the speech itself (I Chr 22 9 Gen 17 5). There is no question of narrative elements being organically related to the formula.

[85] Fichtner op. cit. 381 note 2. Occasionally a birth and naming is reported without the etymology (cf. Gen 4 17a 35 18b 30 21) or with an obscure word play (e. g. probably Gen 38 30. Cf. on this passage, F. Zimmermann, "The Births of Perez and Zerah," JBL 64, 1945, 337f.).

[86] Strictly speaking, Gen 29 34. 35 30 6 show a mixed form. These are treated in detail in a separate discussion.

41 51. 52. Other examples of Form I, with very restricted narrative, report place names: Gen 26 32-33a and I Sam 7 12.

The characteristic feature of all the passages with minimal narration is that the narrative material outside the formula functions neutrally with respect to Form I. It in no way suggests or motivates the name to be given, but rather provides an appropriate setting in which a name may arise. The formulaic structure shows the typical characteristics of Form I summarized above. Briefly, the elements of the simplest report are the following:

(1) Setting
(2) Naming (Form I with β and γ elements, or β alone, in which case the motivation with word play precedes the name)

b) The material

In the case of Gen 3 20, the full formula appears. The explanation of the name is given solely in the typical assonantal word play within the formulaic structure. If there ever existed a narrative setting for this note, it is no longer visible, for the verse ill fits the place given it in the present literary block[87]. In any case, this example represents the very simplest way of reporting an etymological etiological tradition. The narrative function of the formula is prominent here. The definite subject of ויקרא and the absence of narrative material rule out understanding the Form I to be drawing an inference.

In I Chr 4 9, Form I appears as one of a series of loosely joined reports regarding Jabez (v. 9a. 9b. 10)[88]. Narrative continuity can only be read into the text[89]. Assonance is sounded in the β and γ elements. Again, the narrative force of Form I is clear. The thrust lies in reporting the naming and supplying a reason for it.

In Gen 29 31—30 24, the redactor has provided a very general narrative framework by using conventional motifs (strife between wives; a barren wife; gaining of children by a slave)[90]. These motifs are not integral to one name giving situation, but function as a vague context for a whole series of birth reports. Hence the various etymologies are able to stand quite independently of this framework (29 32. 33 30 8. 11. 13. 20. 24). Even the more developed narrative ma-

---

[87] Cf. Gunkel, Genesis, 23; von Rad, Genesis, 93 et al.

[88] קראה appears instead of ותקרא in the formula.

[89] Cf. for example, Curtis, Chronicles, 107, and earlier, I. Benzinger, Die Bücher der Chronik, 1901, 15.

[90] Cf. the commentaries for the source analysis. A recent attempt at history of tradition: S. Lehming, Zur Erzählung von der Geburt der Jakobssöhne, VT 13 (1963), 74—81.

terial in 30 14-16 is very roughly joined to a name etiology (in v. 17-18)
which reports a birth and a name whose explanation goes in quite
a surprising direction[91]. Thus, the birth schema in these two verses
seems independent of the "mandrake story." What is visible in the
larger block (Gen 29 31—30 24) are a number of birth schemata, likely
deriving from both J and E sources, loosely linked together, and
standing quite independent of the narrative material outside the
schemata themselves.

Gen 4 25, which follows abruptly on Lamech's speech, is linked
to the prior literary context only by עוד and a reference to the
Cain-Abel story[92]. The piece, a birth schema A., is remarkable for
its complete lack of relationship to the surrounding traditions. The
subject of Adam's offspring is disturbing in the context of a listing
of the distant descendants of Cain (4 17ff.), and certainly separate
from the new genealogy beginning in 5 1. Therefore, 4 25 probably
should be seen as a fragment of a variant genealogical tradition,
which by nature shows only minimal narrative characteristics (cf.
Gen 5 6ff. and 4 17-22) and which often includes a birth schema. In
this sense, 4 25 is comparable to 5 29, another passage classified as
simple Form I report. Both verses are independent of narrative
material outside the schematic framework of the form.

Gen 41 50-52 are generally taken as a later insertion into the
original Joseph story of chapter 41[93]. Birth schema A. is visible here,
although the report of the birth itself varies slightly from the usual
pattern. Form I[94] (v. 51. 52) shows no clear relationship to narrative
material outside the schema. The birth tradition is a remark germaine
to the theme of Joseph's rise in fortune, but hardly an original part
of the story surrounding it[95].

In all these examples (in Gen 29 and 30 4 25 5 29 41 51f.), the
β element of Form I simply reports the giving of a name. As in the
cases of the simplest occurrence of the Form I (Gen 3 20 I Chr 4 9),
the γ elements — when they appear — are grammatically subordinate
to the report of name giving (Gen 4 25 5 29 41 51. 52 29 32). Following the narration of the giving of the name, the γ element refers for
the first time to the event (in these cases a speech) which is logically
prior to the act of naming, and which gives rise to the name itself.

---

[91] Verses 14-16 are usually assigned to J, v. 17-18 to E. Cf. the commentaries.
[92] Gunkel, Genesis, 54, and generally among commentators.
[93] Ibid. 439. Cf. Skinner, Genesis, 471; P. Volz and W. Rudolph, Der Elohist als
Erzähler: Ein Irrweg der Pentateuchkritik? 1933, 159; lately, L. Ruppert, Die
Josephserzählung der Genesis, 1965, 70 and 86f.
[94] Verse 52 is modified because of the close relationship with the preceding verse.
The Qatal verb functions as a historical tense just as does the ויקרא normally.
[95] Cf. von Rad, Genesis, 373.

This causal relation is clear because γ contains a subordinating expression (כי or לאמר) and a key word which is assonant with the name given to the child[96]. The substance of the word play varies, however. In three instances the key word is a verb describing a divine action (4 25 41 51. 52); once it is the direct result of divine action (29 32); once a verb descriptive of the future role of the child (5 29). Such variations only illustrate the nearly inexhaustible range of possibilities open to the story teller.

The remaining seven cases of Form I (29 33 30 8. 11. 13. 18. 20. 24) occur as a part of birth schema C. Hence a speech which gives rise to the name and which contains a key word assonant with the name, is reported before the act of naming. These quoted speeches substitute for a γ element insofar as they report the motivation for a particular name. There is a significant variation, however. The quoted speeches of schema C. are not grammatically subordinate to the report of the name giving. Rather, they have a syntactically independent status, for the saying uttered at the time of birth is reported alongside other narrative material in a simple coordinate style. This means that the causal link between speech and name is not explicit in the syntax. It is clear only in the word play.

Outside of the name formula, the birth schema provides a bare narrative context. For example, in Gen 29 32a, conception and birth are reported immediately prior to the etymological formula: "And so and so conceived and bore a son (daughter) . . ." This is the common pattern when β and γ elements appear (Gen 4 25 5 29 41 50ff.) or when γ is replaced by a speech (Gen 29 33 30 7. 10. 12. 17. 19. 23). Sometimes this minimal context is slightly elaborated by reporting events prior to the birth (30 17. 22), or circumstantial details (5 28 41 50a). In all cases, it is clear that the central event reported is the birth. All else either leads to this event, or flows from it as a direct consequence. The significant point, however, is that this simple narrative material merely provides a setting for the etymological etiological formula. The report, exclusive of the β and γ elements of Form I does not suggest the name to be given. Rather, it reports a situation — and a fitting one at that[97] — in which the name, and therefore its explanation, can arise. One can put the matter otherwise. The

---

[96] The distinctive subordinating functions of *kî* as a causal conjunction and as a particle introducing direct discourse, have merged in Gen 41 51. 52 4 25. Gen 5 29 has לאמר. Gen 29 32 preserves a purely causal *kî*.

[97] In the Ugaritic texts, the motifs of birth and naming are joined together. Cf. text 75:I:28; less clear, 6:30ff. Older Semitic names in fact seem to reflect the immediacy of the birth situation. Cf. J. Stamm, Die akkadische Namengebung, 1939, prgr. 3, pp. 8ff. All this suggests that the report of a birth provides a natural and familiar context for an explanation of a person's name.

context which lends significance to the name given is encompassed entirely by the limits of Form I. The whole, however, is placed in a commensurate setting comprising the wider narrative elements of the birth schema.

Two other passages, which report the naming of places rather than newly born children, illustrate further these general conclusions: Gen 26 32-33a and I Sam 7 12.

1. Gen 26 32-33a

While there are no serious grounds for suspecting the presence of two literary sources in the larger block Gen 26 23-33[98], verses 32-33a seem to reflect a later stage in the growth of the tradition[99]. The following considerations support this judgment:

(a) Verse 32 begins an entirely new report quite unrelated to the preceding story of covenant making. Its only point of contact with the foregoing material is with the last phrase of v. 25, which in itself is but an incidental note. One might also observe that v. 31 sounds rather like an ending (cf. Gen 32 1 Num 24 25 Gen 21 32b). The phrase, moreover, in v. 32 marks a new turn in the narration, and indeed often signals a separate layer of tradition (cf. Gen 15 18 48 20. But see, to the contrary, Gen 30 35 and 33 16).

(b) The variant of this saga (Gen 21 22-33) agrees in setting the events narrated in Beersheba (cf. Gen 26 23. 33b and 21 31. 32)[100]. Therefore, the original tradition is most likely to have been associated with only one place name. Consequently, a second name שבעה, however it is vocalized, would seem to result from a secondary development.

(c) The likelihood of the presence of variant tradition is suggested by the difficulty which the versions reflect in translating שבעה in v. 33a. LXX gives ορκος implying Hebrew שִׁבְעָה (cf. Gen 21 31). Some others, notably Syriac and Vulgate, imply שָׂבְעָה "abundance," attested in Ez 16 49 שִׂבְעַת לֶחֶם. L. Köhler[101] takes MT שָׂבְעָה to mean "abundance" and thus sides with the versions against the LXX[102].

---

[98] Cf. Gunkel, Genesis, 299f.; Speiser, Genesis, 198 et al.

[99] Already the promise motif (v. 24f.) has been recognized as a later development. Cf. Noth, Pentateuch, 58ff., and Westermann, Forschung, 11ff. and 26.

[100] Perhaps Gen 46 1ff. reflect another variant. If so, the location is again given as Beersheba.

[101] L. Köhler in: ZAW 55 (1937), 166.

[102] Cognates in Ugaritic: šb't "satiety" and the verb šb' which refer frequently to drunkenness: 2 Aqht II:6. 20; 2 Aqht I:32. The Accadian verb šebū, "be sated," is used with reference to food and drink, and frequently in the context of rains

One cannot exclude the possibility that ויקרא אתה שבעה is merely a glossing variant upon the preceding story of an oath, especially in light of the etymological word play in the parallel account Gen 21 31. If this were the case, however, the problem of v. 32, which is completely unmotivated by the preceding material, is left unsolved. Understanding שבעה as "satiety" or "abundance" at least has the virtue of explaining the presence of v. 32 in its present place, for the latter can provide the motivation for this particular name. It seems most likely that a variant name tradition, which takes the form of a simplest report, has somehow come into the Beersheba account.

(d) Two etymological formulae appear in v. 33[103]. Etymological motifs are known to pile up (cf. Gen 30 23f. 22 14 for example), although there are no other examples of Form I and II standing side by side (but cf. Gen 32 30. 32 2 23. 24). The fullness in this verse is likely not due to a combination of literary sources, since a connected second source cannot be detected in the whole account. Rather, the presence of two distinct formulae is more likely explained as accretion of variant tradition.

Now if שבעה is rightly understood as "abundance" or "satiety" then it is clear that v. 33a along with v. 32, rather than Form II (v. 33b), is in the later layer of the tradition, since the water motif has a very minor place in the whole complex[104]. Furthermore, in all occurrences of Form II, על־כן draws an inference from an immediately preceding event or speech in a given situation[105]. Now in the passage under examination, v. 32-33a break the pattern, putting unrelated material between premise and conclusion (Form II). Therefore, v. 32-33a are secondary.

Considering v. 32-33a a secondary tradition, therefore, one lays bare a variant report containing typical elements: neutral setting

---

and floods. (C. Bezold, Babylonisch-Assyrisches Glossar, 1926, 263 ff.). The noun šbʻ appears in eighth century Phoenician (Karatepe) in the sense of general prosperity or "plenty." Cf. in Donner and Röllig, Kanaanäische und aramäische Inschriften, 1962—64, vol. I, text 26 A: III, 7. 9 and IV, 7. 9. The phrase is בעלת שבע ותרש "proprietress of plenty and wine."

[103] There are no γ elements, but their omission is fairly frequent in mixed forms. The verb qrʼ, usually in Form II, is absent in MT, although present in LXX[A] and Syriac versions. Commentators are split over which is the original text. Even without the verb, the על־כן phrase functions more as the classic Form II than Form I.

[104] Some further confirmation lies in the fact that Form I originally seems to have been restricted to personal names, and Form II to place names (Fichtner op. cit. 383). Since the Form I type in v. 33a is linked with a place name, its usage here may reflect a secondary development over against a Form II which retains its original usage.

[105] Cf. above 3 ff.

(servants deliver a message)[106]; speech (the message); naming (Form
I without a γ element). The characteristics of the simplest etymological etiological report are now evident. The setting (v. 32a through
חפרו) merely provides a situation — like the birth report — in which
the name may arise. A quoted speech substitutes for a γ element
and directly motivates the name. The word play which makes this
causal relationship clear, however, is not one of assonance. Instead,
the name taken as a substantive expresses an appropriate and nearly
equivalent response to the substance of the servants' message.

2. I Sam 7 12

This verse apparently is one piece with the foregoing material
stemming from the Dtr historian[107]. Like much of the material in
this block (v. 2-17), verse 12 retains some of its original independence.
It lies outside the thematic development visible in v. 2-13. Striking
confirmation appears in the fact that the verse interrupts the stereotyped schematic conclusion to the Dtr victory summary. The customary formula occurs in Jdc 3 29. 30 4 22. 23 8 28 11 33, and belongs
to the redactor's framework[108]. Typically a summary victory is reported and followed by a concluding statement: "And Yahweh (God)
subdued so and so on that day..." Now in I Sam 7, this schema
appears in v. 11 and 13, and is clearly broken by an intruding name
etiology. Moreover, עד־הנה in the direct motivation for the name,
tends in a direction which ill fits the context provided by v. 10f.[109].

As an originally independent bit of tradition[110], v. 12 provides
another example of the simplest etymological etiological report. A
neutral setting is given (v. 12a) along with a full Form I which displays the typical word play between β and γ elements[111].

---

[106] This statement may possibly be linked to the last phrase of v. 25; the connection,
however, is not smoothe, since v. 32 implies that Isaac knew nothing of a well,
and v. 25 has the well dug at the very spot where Isaac built the altar. The similarity of this well report with the series of traditions in 26 18-22 should be noted.
The latter, however, form a unit with a certain climax. Hence there was no original connection to v. 32-33a.

[107] Cf. the commentaries. Lately, Noth, Studien, 54ff.

[108] Cf. Richter, Bearbeitungen, 3ff.

[109] Many commentators emend the text to עֵדָה הוּא כִּי on the strength of Gen 31 48
and Jos 24 27. There is, however, no manuscript support for this reading. Cf. S. R.
Driver, Notes on the Hebrew Text ... of the Books of Samuel, 1960[2], 65.

[110] Noth, Studien, 56 note 3, definitely understands the matter this way.

[111] The γ element instead of being subordinated to β, is a coordinate sentence with
ויאמר. The word play, however, removes any doubt as to its function; it expresses the motivation for the name.

To sum up: the simplest and clearest examples of Form I appear simply as formulae (Gen 3 20 I Chr 4 9) structured so as to report a naming, a name, and its reason. The creation of a Form I report alters this structure in no essential way. A commensurate setting is provided for the name to be given. The latter is narrated and its reason reported, but is never suggested by the narrative setting itself. Put most sharply, Form I shows no functional connections with the narrative material surrounding it.

PART C. ETYMOLOGY OF A MIXED TYPE

1. Overview

Since Form II, at its simplest, is intrinsically related to narrative material, and since Form I shows no such functional connection, it is not surprising that in cases in which the traditions are more complex, a certain mixing of Form I and II characteristics develops[112]. There are a surprising number of mixed cases (twenty-one in all). The mixing occurs in both old and very young literary strata, and is nearly equally distributed among person and place name traditions. The passages show a wide variation in the degree of mixing; they range from cases in which narrative material — as in Form II reports — is organically linked to an etymological formula otherwise like Form I, to occurrences in which the distinctions between the two forms are almost completely lost. Most of the time it is Form I which has been associated with narrative structures similar to various types of Form II material, and which has in the process been altered in its formulaic structure and function.

2. The material

a) Cases of slight mixing

The breakdown of the Form I pattern is visible in a few passages where the typical neutral narrative material is replaced or supplemented by narration integrally related to the simple report of a name giving. As a consequence, the narrative force of the conventional ויקרא or ותקרא is made more ambiguous, and something of inferential על־כן קרא barely begins to be felt.

---

[112] Cf. Fichtner op. cit. 383. He theorized that originally Form I and II were used in quite different circumstances.

1. I Chr 7 21ff.

The Ephramite genealogy is constructed according to the conventional pattern: simple identification of the family, followed by a listing of descendents. (Cf. Gen 10 2ff. I Chr 2 5ff. 2 25ff. 7 2 7 3ff.) Special narrative traditions about specific persons or tribal affairs and customs are easily detected and their limits defined. (Cf., for example, I Chr 2 23 4 9f. 4 39ff. Gen 36 24.) Thus in the case of I Chr 7 21ff., one can separate out v. 21b-23, beginning with the mention of Ezer and Elead, as special narrative tradition, still in the style of a report, but clearly interrupting the regular cataloguing of offspring. This judgment likely explains the curious fact that neither Ezer, Elead, nor Beriah are known in the parallel genealogy in Num 26 35ff. The independent name report, then, may be analyzed as follows:

(a) Setting (raiding of cattle)
(b) Report: The slaying of the two sons (v. 21b)
(c) Reaction reported:
  (1) Mourning (v. 22)
  (2) Birth schema (with Form I) (v. 23)

The typical relationships between the β and γ elements of Form I are visible here in v. 23. The report of conception and birth do not suggest the name to be given; Form I is comprehensible in itself and its narrative force is clear. Some manuscripts and versions even read ותקרא. Now the γ element, as quotation[113], directly motivates the name. Yet its sense is filled out insofar as the γ element is a commensurate descriptive response to the main event reported outside the birth schema, namely, the slaying of the two sons. The association of רעה with this type of event is neither unusual nor accidental. Jdc 9 56-57 20 12 and Ex 32 12 show that רעה may appear naturally in the context of הרג. I Reg 14 10 associates רעה with the loss of offspring. Hence the association in I Chr 7 21ff. explicitly links the name, through its direct motivation, to a narrative element which is crucial to the integrity of the chain of events narrated. The narrative material outside the birth schema, then, is not simply neutral with respect to Form I, for it provides part of the reason for the given name. To this extent, the simple Form I pattern has been altered.

2. Gen 38 27-30

This block, though probably not a literary addition to the bulk of chapter 38, is somewhat independent of the dramatic development

---

[113] The phrase כי ברעה היתה בביתו is incomprehensible unless *kî* introduces direct discourse. Therefore, read with LXX[B], for MT, בביתי.

in v. 1-26, which reaches its climax in a legal judgment (v. 25f. Cf.
Jer 3 11 Ez 16 52)[114]. The etymology of v. 29 in no way depends upon
the Judah-Tamar story for its sense. Rather, v. 27-30 are clearly separate from chapter 39, and at best comprise an epilogue to the main
narrative. Within the small unit, there are no indications of literary
breaks. Indeed, the motifs of childbirth and naming (with etymology)
mostly appear elsewhere already joined together. It is likely, therefore, that v. 27-30 formed an original tradition unit. However, the
intended etymological point in v. 30 is obscure[115]. Yet Form I in
v. 29, along with its narrative context (v. 27-28), can be examined
apart from any connection with v. 30. This procedure, though admit-
tedly unusual, and destructive of an artistic unity, is permissible
only because v. 27-29 upon analysis, yield a pattern analogous to the
simple Form II report.

A setting (v. 27), which is not really neutral, creates the situation
in which the name (perhaps originally both names) can arise. A
speech (v. 29a), substituting for a γ element[116], directly motivates the
name to be given. The motivation and name are linked typically by
assonance[117]. Moreover, the speech-motivation is dependent upon the
details of the birth report (v. 28-29a) as well as the setting (fact of
twins) for its sense. Thus the verses are a tightly constructed unit.
One can say that the name is linked structurally, as opposed to word
play, to important narrative features, and thus the situation is similar
to Form II. The inferential function constitutive of Form II, however, is lacking, though beginning to be felt.

3. Gen 32 2-3

These verses clearly comprise an independent unit between the
preceding Jacob-Laban tradition and the following account of Jacob's
reconciliation with Esau. The inversion of subject and predicate in
v. 2 marks the abrupt change in subject matter. The piece contains
the following constitutive parts:

---

[114] Cf. H. J. Boecker, Redeformen des Rechtslebens im Alten Testament, 1964, 127f.
There are also parallels to the literary device of following a dramatic resolution
with a terse statement of its result. Cf. Jer 28 16f. Dan 5 26f.

[115] Aramaic reconstructions which relate the name Zerah to the detail of "scarlet
thread" are common. Cf. Gunkel, Genesis, 419. Recently, Zimmermann in: JBL 64
(1945), 377f.

[116] Reading with three MSS and versions ותקרא for MT ויקרא.

[117] The usual translation of עליך as "for yourself" is odd. Ordinarily one would
expect the Hebrew to read לך. The causative sense of על may be present. Cf.
Ps 44 23 Gen 16 5 (LXX here translates with εκ σου). Cf. other attempts in Zimmermann op. cit. 377, and A. Guillaume, Paronomasia in the Old Testament,
JSS 9 (1964), 282 ff.

(a) Report
   (1) Meeting along the way
   (2) Speech
(b) Naming

The γ element is absent, but as has been seen elsewhere, the speech immediately before the act of naming substitutes for γ by reporting in coordinate narrative style the motivation for the name. This is made clear by the paronomasia between מחנה and the place name מחנים.

The narrative material preceding the name formula is not, however, neutral. Jacob's speech, which occasions the name of the place, is an immediate response to the meeting. The fact that his utterance is formulated in language entirely commensurate with this event and clearly refers to it (זה), indicates the close relationship between the two narrated events. Thus three elements of the report (meeting, speech, naming) are indissolubly linked together. One sees that the name is tied directly by assonance to the motivation-speech. But the necessary context for understanding the speech is given only in v. 2b. Therefore, the constitutive parts of v. 2b-3 function together to report and explain the name given to the place. At least to this extent, Form I has given way to Form II.

4. I Sam 4 19-22

This passage also shows an alteration in the pattern of Form I. Moreover, it appears at first glance to function etiologically (a full Form I occurs in v. 21), but on closer examination reveals within its structure indications of an altogether different function. This latter may be corroborated independently by a study of the wider tradition context in chapters 4 and 5.

There is no question that v. 19 begins a new thematic unit which extends to 5 1 where the reporting broken off in 4 11 is resumed. The opening of new scenes, and the closing of old, in this large complex are well marked by thematic shifts and grammatical inversions (4 11. 18 [closing of a scene] 4 19 5 1 [openings]) and once by an introductory phrase (4 5). Now v. 19-22 are unified literarily[118]. The only serious reason for doubt arises from the apparently double quotation in v. 21a and v. 22. But this has been discounted by many[119]. It is perhaps

---

[118] The phrase in v. 19b and 21, ומת חמיה ואישה has been taken as a gloss. Cf. for example, Gressmann, Anfänge, 12. 15f., and W. Caspari, Die Samuelbücher, 1926, 73; L. Rost, Die Überlieferung von der Thronnachfolge Davids, 1926, 12f., now reprinted in: Rost, Das Kleine Credo und andere Studien zum Alten Testament, 1965, 128.

[119] Cf. for example, A. Ehrlich, Randglossen zur hebräischen Bibel, 1908—1918, vol. III 183. Recently, Hertzberg, I and II Samuel (ET of German edition of 1956), 50.

reasonable, as will be seen below, to view v. 22 as a narrator's attempt at clarifying v. 21[120]. Basically, however, v. 19-21 (22) remain a unified whole. One may assume that the unit's shape in oral tradition was not greatly different from its present literary form.

These verses comprise a report consisting of the following elements:

(1) Setting (v. 19a)
(2) Report of birth
    (a) Labor
    (b) Nurses' speech
    (c) No answer
(3) Naming (Form I with β and γ elements) (v. 21)

The β element narrates the name giving. The name's direct motivation is expressed by the γ element לאמר ... מישראל and the name Ichabod ("No glory") is understood as a commensurate descriptive response to the speech quoted in γ[121]. Now this speech itself receives an explicit motivation in the causative clause of v. 21b: "because the ark of God had been captured, and because of her father-in-law and her husband"[122]. Verse 22, perhaps to clarify matters, makes it absolutely clear that these phrases modify the mother's utterance and only indirectly relate to the name given to the child. Further, the modifying phrases are linked directly to a narrative feature (v. 19aβ) which reports in similar language the crucial stimulus in the chain of events leading toward the naming of the child. Hence one can rightly say that the particular name is firmly rooted in a rather tightly constructed unit. The etymology therefore diverges from the pattern of Form I, and shares something of the structural features of a Form II simple report.

It is important to note that the particular name does not arise, strictly speaking, from events reported in v. 19-22, i. e., from birth or the circumstances immediately surrounding it, or the nurses' speech of comfort. Most sharply put, the name and its motivation is in reaction to a prior situation only alluded to in the opening clauses of v. 19, and obviously referring to the catastrophe reported in v. 11ff. The fact that emphasis is atypically upon a reason for the utterance

---

[120] The LXX in v. 21 appears not to have understood the word play in the name and hence translated from the context. Cf. P. de Boer, Research into the Text of I Samuel 1—16, 1938, 51. The Greek and Hebrew of v. 22 agree.

[121] On the negative force of אי in the name, cf. Driver, Notes (second edition), 49. Cf. also Hi 22 30 and M. Pope's comments in his Job, 1965, 152f. In Phonecian, אי has the force of German keine. Cf. Donner and Röllig, Inschriften, vol. I, text 13:4 and 14:5.

[122] אל probably has been confused with על. Cf. Gen 20 2 Ps 2 7.

rather than for the name indicates at once the wider reference. In
this sense, what appears to be a report of mixed form, already within
itself betrays a function obvious from its wider context. It illustrates,
as do v. 12-18, a reaction to the loss of the ark[123]. One may suggest,
therefore, that I Sam 4 19-21 (22) offers a clear case of etymological
tradition, using conventional motifs (cf. Gen 35 16-18), functioning
primarily in an altogether different way. Comparable situations, insofar as each make a theological point in relation to received tradition
are seen in the simplest Form I reports of Gen 41 50ff. and I Sam 7 12.

b) Cases of more advanced mixing

A greater mixing of Form I and II characteristics is evident in
several passages of varying ages: Num 11 1-3 11 4-34 13 23f. II Sam
12 25 Gen 26 17-22. A full Form I occurs in each piece. But firm
connections with narrative materials are obvious, and in some cases
the strictly narrative force of the formula has been clearly weakened.
A sixth passage, Gen 35 8, shares even more characteristics of Form II
simple reports.

1. Num 11 1-3

The problems of literary analysis of chapter 11 are formidable
and largely insoluble[124]. From the point of view of the history of
traditions, however, it is reasonably clear that the Taberah tradition
(v. 1-3) once existed quite independently of the themes of manna and
flesh on the one hand (chapter 11) and the ark on the other (10 35ff.).
The joint, as evidenced by its roughness[125], was made only at the
literary stage. Moreover, Noth has argued[126] that the lament (v. 2)
probably belongs to a later stage of the preliterary history, since the
motif belongs generally to the presentation of the wilderness wander-
ings and needs no special motivation, as it gets here, for its appearance. Thus the earliest visible stage of this special unit involves only
v. 1 and 3, a simple report made up of inseparable narrative statements.

---

[123] A striking and consistent difference in the designation of the ark in 4 1-10 and
4 11-22 forces one to see v. 12-22 as a traditional unit. 4 1-10 has ארון ברית
האלהים or ארון (ברית) יהוה (4 3. 4. 5. 6), whereas 4 11-12 has only ארון האלהים.
Of course in v. 19, the use of וכלתו now links v. 12-18 and 19-22 together.

[124] Cf. the commentaries and their disagreements. Most, however, see it as early stuff.

[125] The text of v. 1a is very strange, and perhaps reflects the disturbance of a more
extensive introduction. Verse 4 with its sudden inversion, a shift to בני ישראל
away from the simple עם of v. 1-3, and the clumsy וישבו ויבכו גם, probably
reflects the rough literary joint.

[126] Pentateuch 135f.

The full Form I with typical relationship between β and γ elements is present in v. 3 The γ element, although in typical fashion expressing the direct motivation for the name, is not a quoted speech. Rather, it is a causal clause which summarizes in almost identical words, a crucial event reported in the narrative material in v. 1. Thus the constitutive word play not only appears in β and γ, but also between the name and a key narrated event.

The setting given in v. 1a cannot function neutrally, therefore. Indeed, the fact of the people's grumbling is necessary to motivate Yahweh's reaction, which in turn provides the direct motivation for the name. Hence the name is linked by assonance to a crucial narrative element. The pattern of Form II in which a reported event serves as a basis for an inference is close at hand. The mixing is probably reflected also in the ambiguity of subject for ויקרא in the β element. It can be indefinite, or can refer to the "people" or to "Yahweh." The very uncertainty already shows a departure from the Form I pattern in which the narrative force, with definite subject, was unambiguous.

2. Num 11 4-34

The name tradition in v. 34 belongs to the story of "cravings" in a way that the itinerary of v. 35 does not. Yet the attachment to this place קברת התאוה seems shallow rooted at best. The name of the locale appears only in v. 34, and a word play is on the root אוה which comes elsewhere only in v. 4. This situation suggests that this particular name tradition was grafted on as a kind of framework to earlier material. The roughness of syntax in v. 4 supports this notion. But more importantly, v. 33-34 introduce rather abruptly an entirely new theme: Yahweh sends a plague, and its victims — those who had cravings — are buried at a certain place which receives an appropriate name. However, the "craving" motif, expressed in the people's request for meat (v. 4b. 13. 18f. 20f.) finds its satisfaction, or resolution, as Yahweh promises and delivers a stifling quantity of meat (v. 19-23. 31-32). Therefore, v. 33f. lie outside the main thematic lines, and go their own way. It seems likely, therefore, that this name tradition is younger than its surrounding context[127].

Yet one cannot simply consider v. 33f. as literary insertions. The merger with the "craving" story apparently came in the pre-literary stage, for now v. 33 obviously provides some sort of transition to the name etiology. Thus it is not a question of an independent etiological report here, but rather a secondary layer of tradition which, because of its integration into the older material, is somewhat atypical. How-

---

[127] Ibid. 130.

ever, it assumes a mixed etymological form suggestive of a Form II
simple report. In this guise, an event is reported (v. 33a) along with
a full etymological formula of Form I type, and showing assonantal
β and γ relationships. However, the *ki* clause, insofar as it refers
back to narrative material is not typical of Form I. Even more important, the phrase points to an action (burying) which is only an
implied consequence of those events reported in v. 33. This is precisely the pattern of the *ki* clause where it appears secondarily with
a Form II report (Gen 11 9 21 31). Moreover, the subject of ויקרא
is indefinite. This fact does not necessarily alter the narrative force
of the β element. However, the similarities with Form II in the general report structure and in the *ki* explanatory clause lead to a supposition that the impersonally formulated inference of Form II is
beginning to emerge with some clarity at this point.

3. Num 13 23-24

The problems of literary analysis in Num 13—14 are many and
complex. The tradition resists a thoroughly satisfactory division into
literary sources. It seems reasonably clear that the final shape stems
from P. In chapter 13, the oldest material is contained in v. 17b-24.
26-31, but even here minor accretions have grown up in the tradition[128].
In general, the thematic development is toward rebellion, as the
ambiguity of the spies' report becomes the cause for dispute[129]. In
this context, the Eshkol tradition (v. 24) is of a subordinate and
digressive character. This judgment is confirmed by the striking fact
that neither אשכול nor ענבים occur outside v. 20-24. The continuity
in the larger account hinges instead on the phrase פרי הארץ appearing in v. 20 and 26f. (cf. Dtn 1 25).

The Eshkol tradition itself (v. 23f.) suggests the pattern of Form
II simple report, despite its minor role in the wider context, and its
almost list-like style of reporting. A setting is provided (v. 23a) which
anticipates the name to be given (cf. elsewhere only with Form II;
Gen 26 23. 33 33 17 Ex 15 23 II Sam 5 20). A series of successive
events is then reported. The full Form I appears in v. 24, showing
typical βγ elements and word play[130]. The link to a crucial narrative
element comes between the name, through the γ element, to v. 23aβ
which reports the cutting of the "cluster" (אשכול). Hence the nar-

---

[128] Cf. commentaries; also Noth, Pentateuch, 34 (n. 121) and 15.

[129] This is precisely the focus which Dtn 1 24f. gives to the tradition.

[130] The formulation is atypical. The *waw* conversive ויקרא which sometimes must
be translated with a general subject, gives way to an inverted word order, using
a Qatal form of *qr'* קרא למקום ההוא קרא (S reads קראו). The γ element is introduced by על־אדות instead of causative *ki*.

rative material is not neutral, but is linked clearly to the etymological
formula in a way similar to that of Form II reports. Moreover, the
unusual formulation of v. 24 points rather more to Form II than to
Form I. The subject of *qr'* must be indefinite, also, since the singular
has no referent[131].

4. II Sam 12 24-25

This passage falls into two main parts:

(1) Birth schema[132]: v. 24
(2) Second name tradition: v. 25
    (a) Report of message sent
    (b) Naming (Form I)

There are no signs of a literary break between v. 15b-23 and v. 24. In
the history of traditions they seem to have been related from the
beginning because together they reveal the conventional sequence of
narrative motifs already seen in I Chr 7 21b-23 (misfortune and mourning; comforting the mourner; conception and birth; naming). The
similarity between the I Chronicles passage, and the account of Solomon's birth, is best explained from the supposition that both passages
are built with a conventional sequence of story motifs. (Cf. I Chr 2 24.)
Thus in II Sam 12, v. 15b-23 are naturally followed by the birth
schema of v. 24.

But ויהוה אהבו of v. 24, and the themes in v. 25 lie both outside
the birth schema and the stereotyped motive sequence[133]. Whereas
a name etymology often appears as a part of the birth schema, the
text here moves in a new direction and reports a second name along
with its explanation which is in no direct way related to what has
gone before. The inversion ויהוה אהבו, remarkable because no particular emphasis upon the word Yahweh seems meaningful at this point,
and because it is the only instance of an inverted subject and predicate in the whole block of tradition in 11 2—12 24, indicates a new
direction in the text. Moreover, the sudden roughness of syntax in
v. 25[134], along with a sudden ambiguity in the third person verbal
subjects, point toward the subordinate character of v. 25. Yet this

---

[131] Only S reads קראו. This, of course, may be read as an indefinite construction.
[132] LXX implies ותהר before ותלד. This is the usual phrase. There is no etymological interest expressed in the schema. Such is not necessary to the form.
[133] H. P. Smith, A Critical and Exegetical Commentary on the Books of Samuel,
1899, 326, and K. Budde, Die Bücher Samuel, 1902, 257, among others, understand ויהוה אהבו with v. 25. Commentators disagree, however. Cf. Hertzberg,
Samuel, 317.
[134] Cf. the commentaries on וישלח ביד נתן and various emendations. The MT
reading is possible, however.

second name tradition cannot now be understood as simply a secondary insertion of once independent material into a literary text,
for in itself, it is not fully comprehensible. The antecedents of its
pronouns clearly lie in v. 24 (אהבו and שמו). What is seen here,
rather, is elaboration in the style of a brief report on an existing
tradition of Solomon's birth and naming[135]. Whether or not the elaboration occurred in the pre-literary history of these traditions is
uncertain, and finally irrelevant at this point. What is evident is
that a birth schema (v. 24 to the phrase "and Yahweh loved him")
merely provides a general setting for a second name tradition (v. 25,
including "and Yahweh loved him" of v. 24) to follow.

    The assonantal relationship between β and γ elements is clear[136].
Now the name ידידה must have been understood as "beloved of
Yah(weh)," for the expression is known in early poetry (Dtn 33 12
ידיד יהוה) and paralleled in the Ugaritic divine epithet *ydd il ġzr*[137].
The root and its participial forms are common to Semitic dialects
(cf. in Hebrew, Jes 5 1 Jer 11 15 Ps 127 2 60 7 // 108 7). It is probable, therefore, that in the name itself an allusion to the narrative
element ויהוה אהבו was clear. Already the Syriac and some Latin
versions saw this in adding to the element in MT the words which
implied Hebrew ידידו[138]. If such is a correct understanding of the
matter, it is evident that the name itself is linked directly to an
important narrative feature through the use of synonomous roots (cf.
similar case in Gen 26 20 26 21). Thus already the pattern of Form I
is altered.

5. Gen 26 17-22

    Three reports are set in series in Gen 26 17-22. This block intro-
duces new motifs whose limits are set by such a phrase as מִשָּׁם in
v. 17 and 23. The verses report events in the "Valley of Gerar," in
contrast to simply "Gerar" (v. 6) and "Beersheba" (v. 23). Surely in
the history of traditions they had no original connection with the
surrounding context, for they express quite unrelated themes. Even
the Beersheba tradition here (v. 23 ff.), in contrast to the situation in

---

[135] Hertzberg, Samuel, 317, speaks of an "express addition."

[136] The γ element is atypical since it is linked to β through בעבור or with some
versions בדבר. In any case, causative *kî* is replaced by *b* in the sense of "because."

[137] Text 49:VI:30—31; also 51:VII:46—47; also in Anat pl. X:IV:20 read *šmk mdd
i(l)*. Cf. further, M. Noth, Die israelitischen Personennamen im Rahmen der ge-
meinsemitischen Namengebung, 1928, 149.

[138] D. Englert, The Peshitto of Second Samuel, 1949, 23, speaks of an "ameliorative
addition." It is possible, of course, that the original Hebrew contained ידידו or
perhaps אהבו. In any case my point of a wider context of meaning is made.

Gen 21 22ff., has nothing to do with the theme of strife over water rights as it is expressed in v. 17-22. Yet the reports of naming of three wells are obviously linked to one another, as v. 21 (גם and אחרת), and v. 22 (משם; אחרת; כי עתה) indicate[139]. Verse 18 likely stems from the redactor[140].

Each of these reports is similar to a Form II report, and yet shows also Form I features. Each provides a setting, but only v. 19 could be considered neutral (v. 19-20. 21aα; 22aα). Each reports a direct motivation for the name, whether in a *kî* clause (v. 20. 22) or a preceding reported event (v. 21). The usual pattern of relationship between β and γ, or the latter's substitute, is evident. However, γ refers to narrated material. The name in each case is linked unmistakably to a crucial narrative feature by use of a synonym (v. 20.21)[141] or commensurate descriptive response (v. 22; cf. Gen 26 32-33a). There is little doubt that in each case, the narrative features function as a unit to explain the name, and in a way closely resembling that of Form II.

It is worth noting that first signs of further narrative complexity already appear in this passage. The three reports, though formally somewhat independent of each other, make up a series which has a certain dramatic development issuing finally in the possession of water and living space. This in itself points toward the Form II usage.

6. Gen 35 8

This verse is clearly independent of its context. The appearance of tradition about Deborah, who is unnamed in 24 59, is very abrupt and completely unmotivated by the preceding verses. Like so many

---

[139] Whether or not the reports are each a remnant of a larger saga is not certainly known, and no longer pertinent. The question for present purposes has to do with their characteristics as they stand. For a reconstruction of a saga type, of which the reports are but residue, cf. Westermann, Forschung, 67.

[140] Gunkel, Genesis, 302f.; Holzinger, Genesis, 175; Fichtner op. cit. 381 note 5. But others (Driver, Genesis, 252f.; Speiser, Genesis, 203f. et al.) are not sure. Verses 19-22, however, tell of the naming as if it were for the first time. This tends to confirm the secondary character of v. 18, probably linked to v. 15 somehow.

[141] In v. 20, Hithp. *'śq* is apparently parallel to *rîb*. The word is known from its cognates in the various Semitic languages. It occurs in eighth century Aramaic in the context of *rîb* (cf. Donner-Röllig, Inschriften, vol. I, text 224:20 and 226:8). *Śiṭnā* in v. 21 occurs elsewhere only in Esr 4 6 and refers to a written document, perhaps an "accusation." This is certainly in the context of strife (cf. 4 1). Moreover, the verb *śṭn* is associated in Ps 109 4. 20 with a semantic unit similar to that often connected with *rîb* (Ex 17 2 Num 20 3 Jdc 11 25 Neh 13 25 et al.). Thus at the very least, the verb *'śq* and the word *śiṭnā* are naturally, if not synonymously, associated with *rîb*.

4

8   Etymological Etiologies

grave traditions (e. g. Num 20 1 Dtn 10 6), the note on Deborah's
death and burial was probably occasioned by the mention of a particular locale[142].

Formally, the verse is a compressed piece which shares many
features of Form II reports. Verse 8a simply reports the death of
Deborah. As in Form II, a locale for burial is specifically identified.
The naming follows, formulated with an indefinite subject. There is
no *kî* explanatory clause. Undoubtedly the name is intended to be
a commensurate descriptive response to a customary action, though
unexpressed, of mourning for the dead. Thus the narrative material
in v. 8a provides the situation in which the particular name may
arise, and also implies conventional actions which presumably motivated the name. There is little question, therefore, that the narrative
elements function together to provide a basis for the name.

c) Cases of advanced mixing in developed reports

Two occurrences of the mixed etymological form, both in the
older strata of literary tradition, appear in narrative material similar
to a Form II developed report (Num 21 1-3 Gen 25 21-26). Each
passage shows a thematic development whose climax (or immediate
circumstances surrounding such) motivates the particular name reported by the ויקרא formula without a γ element. Moreover, in each
case, the subject of ויקרא is indefinite as is usual in Form II, and
the inferential force typical for Form II coexists with the narrative
function of *waw* conversive ויקרא.

1. Num 21 1-3

These verses form a finished unit originally independent of its
present literary context and representative of older material in Numbers[143]. It clearly breaks the continuity between 20 22-29 and 21 4
(note "Mount Hor" in 20 22 and 21 4, but not 21 1-3)[144]. The sequence
of motifs, moreover, (vow made; vow fulfilled separately by each
contracting party) because of its conventional rigidity (cf. Jdc 11 29-40
I Sam 1 11-28 Num 30 3. 4ff. Koh 5 3. 4), suggests that the tradition
originated on the oral level in essentially the form in which it now
stands. As such, these three verses comprise a report structurally
similar to the Form II simple report. Events reported in v. 1-2 lead
to the direct motivation for the name, which is narrated in v. 3b;

---

[142] Cf. Noth, Pentateuch, 93, and von Rad, Genesis, 333. Gunkel, Genesis, 379, cor-
rectly saw that v. 8 belonged to the latest stage of the complex v. 1-8.

[143] Noth, Pentateuch, 34.

[144] Cf. the commentators. Overwhelmingly they assign v. 1-3 to the J source. Noth,
Pentateuch, 34, is not as positive.

the relation between this event and the name giving is seen in the assonance between ויחרם and the name חרמה. There is no γ element and the indefinite subject of ויקרא tends toward an inferential על־כן קרא.

What is striking here is the fact that the report shows a dramatic development typical in the Form II developed report. The setting voices a tension created by the warring Canaanite king (v. 1), which is resolved when Israel "utterly destroyed them and their cities" (v. 3). And the means toward that resolution is encompassed by the report of the vow and its fulfillment. Thus the case is not simply that the report consists of three tightly knit narrative elements, but rather that a thematic movement from tension to resolution shapes the piece. More important, perhaps, is the fact that the resolution itself, the final resting point of the report, directly motivates the name to be given. Put another way, the weight of the tradition, its function, i. e., to describe the destruction of the Canaanites, at the same time provides the motivation for and sense to the name of the region[145]. Furthermore the key means to the resolution, the vow, is integrally bound up with the verb *ḥrm* which is to suggest directly by assonance the name to be given. There can be little doubt, then, that these narrative elements function as do the Form II dramatic units, to motivate and explain the name.

2. Gen 25 21-26

In their present form, these verses comprise a loosely woven fabric set in the context of other fragmentary traditions about Esau and Jacob (v. 27-34)[146]. Despite the difficulty in the text of Rebekah's cry (v. 22b)[147], it is reasonably certain that v. 22f. belong together. Yet the prophecy in v. 23 floats somewhat independently of the context provided by v. 24ff. and v. 21. Thematically, it is oriented toward *tribal* tradition (גוים // לאמים cf. Gen 27 29 Jes 34 1 Ps 105 44), whereas the birth narrative (v. 24ff.) is formulated fundamentally to report the birth and naming of *specific persons*[148]. Moreover, plural

---

[145] From its context here, מקום probably has a wider connotation (although the name, Hormah, in Jdc 1 17 refers to a city). Cf. Ex 23 20 and I Sam 12 8, and G. Gray, A Critical and Exegetical Commentary on Numbers, 1903, 273.

[146] These verses are now framed by priestly tradition in v. 19-20 and 26bβ ("and Isaac was 60 years old when she bore them"). Verses 21-26bα then are J. Cf. Gunkel, Genesis, 293ff.; Speiser, Genesis, 193ff., and commentaries in general.

[147] Most translators follow the Syriac, which may itself reflect nothing more than a correction of a corrupt MT, adding חַיָּה: "if it is like this, why do I live?" (Cf. Gen 27 46.)

[148] The narrator and audience undoubtedly were aware that tribal ancestors were being talked about. But this supposition should not blur the actual characteristics

הבנים in v. 22 presupposes a situation which is only first reported
in v. 24 by means of a typical circumstantial clause (cf. Gen 38 27
Gen 24 30). It is likely, therefore, that v. 22f. were originally independent and were joined, probably at the literary stage in the history of
tradition, to the report of the birth of Esau and Jacob[149]. If so,
v. 21. 24-26 bα may be examined as a literarily separate unit. Furthermore, there is every reason to believe that these verses originated in
oral tradition in nearly their present form, for the narrative motifs
of barren wife and birth-naming frequently appear joined together
in a dramatic sequence. (Cf. the skeletal outline of Jdc 13 2. 24 and
I Sam 1 2. 20; a more formulaic witness in Gen 29 31f. and 30 22f.;
implicit sequence in Gen 21 1ff. 20 17f.)

Now the piece v. 21. 24-26 bα, a considerably elaborated birth
schema B., reveals some characteristics of a Form II simple report.
The etymological formula appears in v. 25 b and 26 bα; in each case the
subject is indefinite. There is no γ element. The direct motivation as
shown by the assonantal word play is narrated prior to the formula.
One feels, therefore, something of the inferential force of the formulation. There is also evident a dramatic development. The setting
which was neutral in the Form I simplest reports now gives expression to a point of tension which is only resolved, through plea and
responsive divine action, in the event of birth. The thematic movement from tension to resolution, paralleled in Form II developed
reports, constitutes the whole of the report. But at the same time,
this resolution and the circumstances surrounding it, provide the
motivation and therefore etymological sense for the particular names
given to the newly born sons. Furthermore, v. 24, a narrative element
which, strictly speaking, lies somewhat outside the barest possible
line from tension to resolution, provides detail crucial to the understanding of the birth situation. Thus the whole report — even with
its rather detailed description of the birth event — is a tightly constructed unit which leads to the motivation and therefore explanation
of the names.

d) Cases of advanced mixing in narrative

There are two occurrences of a mixed form in the midst of
material similar in structure to the Form II narrative. Each appears
in the J document and deals with personal names (Gen 19 37f.

---

of a birth report, so that one sees only poorly disguised tribal history. An analogous situation is in Gen 29 31—30 24, where tribal ancestors are spoken of in
quite specific, personal terms. Cf. von Rad's comments in his Genesis, 291f.

[149] Westermann, Forschung, 78f., on slightly different grounds, reaches the same
conclusion.

2 23). They each show the same ambiguity of form and function as other mixed passages. Here, however, these complex narratives consisting of two well marked dramatic scenes, do not function primarily to explain a name. At best the etymological interest helped to shape the narrative lines.

1. Gen 19 30-38

There is general agreement that Gen 19 30-38 is a literary unit, probably from J, and certainly originally was independent of its present context[150]. Its present connection with Zoar (v. 30a; cf. v. 22) is likely secondary in the history of the tradition, as the somewhat repetitive and full setting in v. 30 shows[151]. But the artistic balance of the piece suggests that it became fixed in tradition early, and one cannot with much certainty push further.

Yet for the question of etymological function, there are difficulties. Verse 37 contains no γ element, and v. 38 seems to have lost a name but retained its explanation (בן־עמי). The basis for this judgment lies only in the divergent Greek readings. Form I appears in v. 37 and 38. All Greek manuscripts in v. 37 following Hebrew מואב add λεγουσα εκ του πατρος μου[152]; and v. 38 reads in the Greek: και εκαλεσεν το ονομα αυτου Αμμαν υιος του γενους μου[153]. Commentators have been at odds whether or not to accept the LXX reading as superior[154]. Since for v. 30-36 the Greek implies, with very minor divergencies, the present MT, it seems likely that such a γ clause and the name, Ammon, were at one time in the Hebrew version. In such a case, both v. 37 and 38 contain a typical example of Form I with β and γ elements. The latter, as shown by the first person possessive pronoun (πατρος μου and γενους μου) are quoted speeches which directly motivate the particular names. The familiar assonantal relationships between β and γ are obvious.

Yet the piece shares features of Form II, notably a structural unity:

(1) Tension: v. 31
(2) Towards resolution:
   v. 32-33
   v. 34-35
(3) Conception: v. 36

---

[150] Cf. the major commentaries.

[151] Cf. Gunkel, Genesis, 217, who sees a literary insert in v. 30a.

[152] Implying Hebrew לאמר מאבי.

[153] There are a few minor variants in the spelling of *Amman*. A few MSS add λεγουσα after *Amman*.

[154] Contrast for example Gunkel, Genesis, 220, and Procksch, Genesis, 133.

(4) Resolution of the tension (birth):
   v. 37 (Form I)
   v. 38 (Form I)

There are no neutral narrative elements, for the etymological formulae clearly are integrally bound up with them. The tension created,
as v. 31 gives it, by childless daughters in a nearly male-less world,
is resolved only in the birth of sons in v. 37f. And naming, more often
than not, was immediately associated with the event of birth. Moreover, the γ elements effectively capsulate the means toward this
resolution: "from my father" (note the role which "father" plays in
the narrative: v. 31. 32². 33². 34². 35. 36) or "son of my kinsman." In
short, the γ speeches are commensurate descriptive responses to the
bulk of the narrative complex (v. 32-35). As responses, they employ
synonym (עם)¹⁵⁵ and nearly identical phraseology (מאבינו v. 32. 34).
Already much of the Form II pattern is evident.

   Obviously, one must speak here of a *narrative*. The characteristics found typical for developed reports are visible but considerably
broadened. Conversation appears (v. 31-32. 34), scenes are played out
(v. 31-33. 34-35), and narrative third person "reports" are integrated
into the whole (v. 33. 35. 36ff.). Moreover, the analysis has demon-
strated that the etymological etiological formulae are organically related to the entire piece.

   Yet one cannot overlook the fact that the etymologies are not
the final item in the unit. The laconic concluding formula ("He is the
father of . . . to this day.") appearing both in v. 37 and v. 38, prohibit
understanding the function of the whole solely in terms of etymology.
These phrases, since they clearly modify the persons named, establish
a continuity between the tribes of the present (Moabites and Am-
monites) and the sons of Lot. There is little indication, especially in
light of the balanced structure of the piece, that the "extension"
formulae are secondary in the tradition. It seems, rather, more likely
that interests which often are expressed independently of one another
(e. g., origin of tribes or tribal characteristics [Gen 9 18b 4 20f.] and
name etymologies), already at the earliest visible stage have been
fused together. Thus at best, one can say that the etymological interests helped shape the narrative; the clear relational lines between
narrative elements and the name formula indicate as much. But the
etymology is subordinate to the wider interest expressed sharply by

---

[155] Hebrew עם (v. 38) is not to be translated "people" but rather as a male relative,
   a "paternal kinsman." Speiser, Genesis, 144, renders "son of my kin." Greek
   γενος translates עם in this more specific sense here and in Gen 25 17 35 29, the
   conventional death announcement: "he was gathered to his kinsmen."

the "extension formulae." The whole piece drives toward tribal origins rather than name explanations.

2. Gen 2 18-24 (J)

This piece is a thematic unit separable on the one hand from v. 15-17 and on the other hand from v. 25 which introduces a new traditional motif[156]. There are certain signs of sifting within this unit. The LXX reads only Θεος in v. 19. 21 for Hebrew יהוה אלהים[157]. Verse 19b is grammatically disturbed and almost a doublet of v. 20. A broader subject, involving new vocabulary, is suddenly introduced in v. 24. However, the evidence does not decisively argue against seeing an essentially unified whole[158]. Perhaps the roughness in composition derives from a now obscure pre-literary history.

The piece is carefully built:

(1) Tension: v. 18
(2) Towards resolution: v. 19-20
    Creation of animals
    Bringing them to the man
    Naming
(3) Resolution: v. 21-23
    Creation of woman
    Bringing her to the man
    Name stipulated
(4) Derivation of sexual attraction: v. 24

One sees immediately that the material goes beyond a developed report in complexity because of the two clearly demarcated scenes (v. 19-20. 21-23) united in the movement from tension to resolution.

Now the name tradition in v. 23 offers a modification of the typical Form I. The act of naming is not narrated, but stipulated in a curiously rhythmic speech using the Niphal of qr'. However, generally speaking, the stipulation functions similarly to the usual β element. A kî causal clause follows and expressly presents the direct motivation for the name.

But with respect to this etymological formula, the narrative material does not function neutrally. Not only is the naming of woman expected in the structural scheme of the whole piece (all the animals receive their names from the man), but the kî clause in the

---

[156] Cf. Gunkel, Genesis, 11 ff., and von Rad, Genesis, 82 ff., and others.
[157] W. Eichrodt, Die Quellen der Genesis von neuem untersucht, 1930, 199 ff., summarizes the problem and its solutions in the wider context of the whole chapter.
[158] Cf. to the contrary, C. A. Simpson, Traditions, 53 ff.

formula as speech is commensurate descriptive response to a crucial event reported, i. e., the creation of woman. Thus the name itself is organically related to the bulk of the preceding narrative. Again the patterns of Form II are near at hand.

Verse 24, however, is not to be taken lightly. By drawing an inference from the resolution of the narrative, i. e., the creation of woman from man, the whole piece is given a larger function than simply explaining a name. There are no strong reasons for doubting the verse's originality here. So again, as with Gen 19 30-38, one is confronted by a narrative which was probably shaped in part by an etymological interest, but which functions in an altogether different way. The story drives toward an explanation of sexual attraction rather than name.

e) Cases of very advanced mixing

There are five occurrences of etymological formulae in which the distinctions between Forms I and II have almost disappeared. A grammatical formulation characteristic of Form I (ויקרא) now functions entirely as על־כן קרא of Form II in Jos 5 9 and II Sam 6 8. The opposite is the case in Gen 29 34. 35 30 5f.

The latter is clear because to all appearances the material here conforms to the pattern of a Form I simplest report. In Gen 29 34. 35 the birth schema provides a neutral setting in which the mother's utterance may motivate the child's particular name. Then follows the report of the naming[159]. In terms of function these two verses are paralleled exactly by Gen 29 33, a Form I report. Yet v. 34. 35 read על־כן קראה instead of the usual ותקרא[160]. It is clear, therefore, that the inferential function of על־כן, so characteristic of Form II, has given way almost completely to the narrative force of a finite verb with a definite subject in a specific time.

In the case of Gen 30 5f. there is no narrative material intrinsic to the etymology of v. 6. In fact the name tradition (Dan, v. 6b) and its motivation (v. 6aα) only loosely fit the preceding dialogue. The Dan tradition rests in a certain tension with v. 6aβ, which appears to be a conventional explanation for a name (cf. Gen 29 33 and 30 22) but lacks the paronomasia with the name Dan. It is likely, therefore, that the Dan tradition, now a fragmentary birth schema C., once was independent of its present context. As such, it conforms to the pattern of the simplest Form I report: a name and its speech-motiva-

---

[159] Cf. above 30 ff.

[160] In verse 34, קרא should be read with S and most versions קראה. One MS of the Targum even has ותקרא.

tion is reported. Here again, the etymological formula, while suggestive of Form II (עַל־כֵּן קָרָא שְׁמוֹ), functions primarily as *narration*,
and thus parallels the Form I usage of וַתִּקְרָא.

An opposite sort of mixing is apparent in Jos 5 9. The fact that
an interpretation of the quoted speech in this verse is so difficult,
already indicates the imprecision of any connection with the preceding narrative materials. The new theme is only very loosely related
to the subject of circumcision (5 2-8)[161], and was likely independent
of its present context. The verse may of course be a remnant of
another narrative tradition, perhaps connected with 5 1, or it may
reflect a later accretion to the circumcision account. In any case, the
etymological formula in v. 9, while cast like Form I (וַיִּקְרָא שֵׁם),
functions inferentially as does Form II. The adverbial modifier, "as
at this day," demands an indefinite subject for וַיִּקְרָא, and makes
clear that the name clause is drawing an inference applicable into
the narrator's time. Hence the strictly narrative function of the verb
in Form I has broken down.

Similarly, with II Sam 6 8. This verse apparently is not a literary
insertion into the history of the ark[162]. But there are grounds for
suspecting it to be younger than the surrounding materials. For one
thing, David's reaction to the same event, i. e., the death of Uzzah,
is given twice: once in v. 8 (anger), and a second time in v. 9 (fear).
Now v. 8 appears to have arisen later than the tradition of Uzzah
and the ark because it disturbs a conventional sequence of motifs
(Yahweh's anger, his punishment; a fearful reaction accompanied by
repentance, pleas, laments or the like. Cf. Num 12 9ff. 11 1-3 Jdc
10 7ff. II Reg 13 3ff. Ps 106 40ff. Jos 7 1ff.). The name tradition[163]
is at best a subordinate motif secondary to the original ark story[164].

As secondary, or perhaps only subordinate tradition, the verse
shows the וַיִּקְרָא formulation functioning as עַל־כֵּן קָרָא. The verb
is modified by "until this day" and hence must be translated with
an indefinite subject and understood as a conclusive clause. Again,
the Form I features have nearly given way to a Form II inferential
function. This conclusion is indicated already by the absence of a
neutral setting typical of the Form I pattern.

---

[161] Childs, JBL 82 (1963), 285. Noth, Studien, 39, speaks of an "etiological remark."

[162] Cf. the commentaries, and especially Rost, Thronnachfolge, 129, who takes chapter 6 to be largely a literary unity.

[163] I Chr 13 9 reads גֹּרֶן כִּידֹן for II Sam 6 6 גֹּרֶן נָכוֹן. This fact has been used to
support the hypothesis of a version which played upon a verb *kîd*.

[164] The direct motivation, though clear because of the word play, is atypical. It is
formulated as a subordinate clause rather than as a quoted speech or reported
event in coordinate style. This fact may in itself indicate that the verse is not
integrally linked to its wider narrative surroundings.

PART D. SUMMARY AND CONCLUSIONS

The study of etymological formulae and their associated narrative contexts has yielded a fundamental distinction between Fichtner's Form I and II. The former is in no constitutive way linked with narrative material, and the latter shows a basic narrative structure organically related to the name formula as is premise to conclusion. A large body of material shares in varying degrees characteristics of both Form I and II.

In no case is the etymological interest a focal point for extensive traditions. In their most complex occurrences (Gen 19 37f. Gen 2 23), the Mixed Forms are subordinated to a narrative interest other than etymology. The two cases of genuine Form II narrative (Gen 11 1-9 26 23-33) are anecdotal in length. Most of the time, etymological etiology is expressed by formulae (Form I), or short reports (Form II or Mixed Form) in secondary or at least subordinate layers of tradition. Thus great caution is demanded in speaking of etymological etiological *narrative*. An example of such is quite rare.

APPENDIX TO SECTION I

There are several occurrences of etymological formulae where the isolating of surrounding narrative material from its wider context cannot decisively be carried through on the basis of literary and tradition-history criticism. In such cases, the application of criteria developed thus far in this above investigation brings a measure of clarity to the problematic analysis. Such application, of course, can in no way demonstrate the validity of these criteria. The procedure merely shows something of their utility in shifting the balance of probabilities in those cases where an investigator lacks reasonably certain grounds for deciding what narrative elements in a given complex originally functioned integrally with the etymology.

The problematic passages have to do with the names of persons (Ex 2 10 2 22 I Sam 1 20), places (Gen 28 19 Jdc 2 5 15 17) and objects (Jdc 6 24). When subjected to analysis, most of them reduce to the pattern of a Mixed Form report, which assumes a subordinate role in its wider narrative context.

1. Ex 2 10

The story of Moses' adoption (v. 1-10) has frequently been analyzed in terms of J and E by commentators. Very recently the at-

tempt has been made again[165]. A more reasonable view in my opinion, since positive signs of J or E are absent, is to assume that old
material (likely J?) has undergone various expansions. In this case,
the several inconsistencies (e. g., the introduction of an older sister in
v. 4f. 7, whereas v. 1f. imply that Moses is the first born) are best
explained, especially since they do not form a connected narrative
in themselves[166]. The resulting picture is that v. 1-3. 5-6. (9?). 10aβ-10b
represent the oldest visible layer of the tradition (v. 4 and 7f. 10aα
through הילד are expansions). It is no accident, then, that very old
traditional motifs which are deeply rooted in ancient near eastern
culture, appear in just these few verses[167].

Form I appears in v. 10b and shows a typical assonantal word
play. The question is whether or not this name etymology is organically connected with the older layer. There are no signs of a literary
break. B. S. Childs has argued, with good reason, that the traditional
background of the motifs used in the account makes it highly unlikely that the narrative focused on an explanation of Moses' name[168].
However, the etymology offered fits in a general way some of the
action in the story. Thus Noth is undecided[169]. In terms of the thematic development of these verses, the tension created when the babe
is abandoned is only finally resolved at the point of adoption (v. 10aβ).
Now naming seems naturally enough to be concomitant with the
legal act of adoption. Yet to my knowledge, there is little evidence
that naming and adoption were joined in tradition in the way that
birth and naming were linked[170]. Therefore the possibility is at least
open that the naming of Moses is secondary to an original adoption
tradition. In any case, the former is subordinate to the thematic
lines from tension to resolution.

Now the name tradition in v. 10b certainly conforms to the pattern of the Form I simplest report. A neutral setting is provided
(v. 10a); direct motivation for the name is expressed in a classic γ

---

[165] Cf. G. Fohrer, Überlieferung und Geschichte des Exodus, 1964, 18ff. Less recently,
Beer, Exodus, 19f. The earlier commentators saw mostly E with J influence or
vice versa.
[166] Noth, Pentateuch, 31; Exodus, 25. Cf. also B. S. Childs, "The Birth of Moses,"
JBL 84 (1965), 109ff.
[167] Cf. earlier H. Gressmann, Mose und seine Zeit, 1913, 1ff., and the recent correc-
tions by Childs op. cit. The traditional adoption procedure makes it probable
that the wet nurse motif (v. 9) belongs with the oldest stratum of tradition.
[168] Childs op. cit. 116.
[169] Exodus 26.
[170] The only possible Old Testament text which might possibly show their connection,
other than Ex 2 10, is Ruth 4 16, and this is very doubtful. Extra-biblical evidence
likewise is very meagre.

element. Yet, something of the Form II *simple* report structure is
also visible here, for the name is related through its motivation to a
narrative feature which describes the rescue scene (v. 5f.). But this
relation is at best very loose, and really ill fitted. The quoted γ element speech has Pharaoh's daughter "drawing" the babe from the
water, whereas v. 5f. only imply such an act. Neither מים nor משה
appear here. And only by a further logical extension could one say
that the princess herself fetched the child. The γ element, then, is
loosely descriptive of an implicit action in the narrative material.
There is neither paronomasia nor synonym expressed. It seems doubtful, therefore, that the formula as it appears here functions as an
integral part of the whole tradition. Therefore the etymology is best
understood as a part of a Form I simplest report, subordinate to the
main narrative, and perhaps modeled in part on the pattern of
Form II reports.

2. Ex 2 22

This verse is judged by most commentators to be a part of the
literary block v. 11-14 (15). 16-22 (J)[171]. Noth[172] has argued that the
"Gershom" tradition is a bit of northern material (Gershom is the
traditional ancestor of the Danite priests; cf. Jdc 18 30) which was
linked up with the figure of Moses in the later development of the
Pentateuch. Now v. 22 is a typical example of the birth schema
simplest Form I report[173]. The motivation for the name, however,
shows only a highly generalized link with the preceding material.
Neither גר nor גור appear outside the γ element. Hence there is no
assonance between name and narrative. The element does not express
an obvious synonym to a specific word in v. 16-21. Moreover, the
name is not given as a descriptive response commensurate with a
specific narrative element. Rather the speech-motivation is a comment on the general situation of Moses in Midian. It is a proposition
illustrated in the account, rather than being one derived from the
story's development. Therefore, originally the "Midian" tradition
seems to have functioned separate from the etymology[174], and thus
the latter has retained its essentially pure Form I characteristics.

---

[171] Cf. the major commentaries.

[172] Exodus 37; also his Pentateuch 202 f.

[173] Some MSS read for MT ויקרא the more usual ותקרא. The LXX adds further
elements of the birth schema.

[174] The unmotivated choice of Midian as the locale for Moses' flight shows that the
account was likely connected with the theophany tradition in chapter 3 rather
than to an explanation of a name.

3. I Sam 1 20

This verse comes in the midst of a much larger tradition complex extending over 1 1—4 1a whose point is expressed in 3 19-21[175]. Most critics agree that the redactor's hand is visible in 2 35f. and in the insertion of 2 1-10. Chapter 1 falls into four distinct parts: (a) the setting (v. 1-8); (b) the vow (v. 9-18); (c) God keeps bargain (v. 19f.); (d) Hannah keeps bargain (v. 21-28). There is little question that this material passed into the Dtr history already unified[176]. The strongest support for this judgment comes from a study of the vow motif. As v. 11ff. show, a report (ותדר נדר) introduces a quotation consisting of a protasis (אם plus emphatic infinitive plus finite verb) and apodosis (first person finite verb plus simple *waw*). This quoted speech governs the shape of the narration to follow, for each party implicated in the vow (God and Hannah) fulfills his obligation. Yahweh "remembers" Hannah and she bears a son (v. 19f.), and Hannah "gives" the boy to Yahweh (v. 21-28). The movement from vow to complete satisfaction constitutes the story. Precisely the same pattern appears in Num 21 1-3 and Jdc 11 30-39. (Cf. also Gen 28 20-22 and the fulfillment in 35 1-7; also Num 30 3f. and Koh 5 3f.; further in Ugaritic, *Krt* 200ff.) In light of the conventional motive sequence, I Sam 1 11-28 appears to have been a unified whole in its earlier history. This means further that the birth schema and etymological Form I in v. 20 must be seen as a subordinate motif within the vow schema. It lies outside the thematic lines which reach their completion in v. 28.

From the point of view of the criteria for etiological report, a similar conclusion is indicated. At the very least, v. 20 conforms to the pattern of a simplest Form I report on the occasion of birth[177]. The name is related through its motivation only loosely to a crucial narrative element. The verb שאל is in a very general way descriptive of the action described in v. 9-11. Yet the latter section obviously is an important element in the thematic structure of the whole. On the other hand, the strongest link between name and narrative material appears in Eli's dismissal speech (v. 17) in which Hannah's action is explicitly described as "making a petition" (שלתך אשר שאלת)[178]

---

[175] Noth, Studien, 60f. Cf. also Hertzberg, Samuel, 43f.

[176] Even such a radical critic as Gressmann found only a few secondary accretions. Cf. his Die älteste Geschichtsschreibung und Prophetie Israels, 1910, 1f.

[177] The opening phrase of v. 20 is troublesome. The singular (with some MSS) is probably correct. Some critics place it just before v. 21. (So Ehrlich, Randglossen, III 166; J. Wellhausen, Der Text der Bücher Samuelis, 1871, 37f., and followed by many.) The LXX breaks the conventional Hebrew formula.

[178] Many MSS read שְׁאֵלָתֵךְ. Cf. GK² 23f.

thus making a word play on שמואל as does the quoted speech-
motivation (v. 20b). But Eli's blessing (cf. 2 20) is a minor motif in
the overall structure and even within v. 9-20. What is missing here is
a tight structure whose elements in their logical interrelationships
drive inexorably toward the particular name. The fact that the final
resolution of v. 1-28 does not actually motivate the name giving (even
though v. 27f. may contain word plays on Samuel's name and may
relate to the vow itself)[179] reveals immediately that v. 20 did not
provide the focus for the surrounding complex. At best, the etymology
appears here in a Form I simplest report, and perhaps helped v. 12-18
gain its present form by providing the suggestion for Eli's speech.

4. Gen 28 19

This verse falls clearly in the midst of a complex block of tradition given in v. 10-22. Because of numerous doublets, there is substan-
tial agreement that a J version partially preserved in v. (10).13.15.16.19
is now overlaid and dominated by an E account (v. 11-12.17-18.20-22)[180].
Both versions speak of a dream theophany: E explicitly (v. 12) and
J implicitly (v. 16). But only the J fragment contains an example of
an etymological formula[181]. Verse 19b is probably a gloss[182].

Now the etymology, appearing in v. 19a, seems to be directly
motivated by Jacob's speech reported in v. 16b. The name given to
the place represents a commensurate descriptive response to the substance of a speech. There is no γ element. Thus the occurrence of the
name giving here, while similar to Form I, is close to the pattern of
Form II simple report. Further conclusions may be drawn only with
difficulty. It does not appear, however, that a direct link remains
between name and crucial narrative elements outside the simplest
report schema. The chief difficulty is that the J tradition is frag-

---

[179] On the speculation that at one time the story was linked to Saul (cf. שָׁאוּל in
v. 28), cf. I. Hylander, Der literarische Samuel-Saul-Komplex, 1932, 13 ff. In my
opinion, the state of the text offers little firm support for such an hypothesis.

[180] Cf. Noth, Pentateuch, 30 f. 38 f.; Simpson, Traditions, 97; Speiser, Genesis, 217 f.
Cf. E. L. Ehrlich, Der Traum im Alten Testament, 1953, 27—32. Also, C. Keller,
Über einige alttestamentliche Heiligtumslegenden, ZAW 67 (1955), 141—168; 68
(1956), 85—97.

[181] That the interest of E lay elsewhere is shown by the absence of a clear naming
formula and by the E reflections (Gen 31 13 35 1-7) which effectively reduce the
tradition to its cultic significance in conjunction with Jacob's vow and its fulfillment. Even in 28 1ff., the vow tradition exists in some tension with the story
elements preceding. (E. g., v. 17 has the place referred to as the house of God,
whereas in v. 22, the pillar is given this designation.)

[182] Ehrlich, Traum, 27; Noth, Pentateuch, 30 f. Cf. Gen 35 6 Jdc 1 23 Jos 18 13
Gen 48 3.

mentary, and dominated now by the promise motif which certainly is not directly related to the name or its explanation. Yet the name given is commensurate with the action reported in v. 13a (theophany) and the name's motivation comes in a speech which is a stylized reaction to the theophany (cf. Jdc 6 22 13 22 Gen 16 13b Ex 20 18f. Dtn 5 24ff.). Insofar as these elements are linked together, something of the Form II simple report structure remains. Thus, v. 19a appears to be a Mixed Form. The more complex relationships visible in developed etymological reports are obscured if they once were present.

5. Jdc 2 1-5

Despite the disagreements over the literary relationships between Joshua and Jdc 1 1—2 5 and Jdc 2 6ff., it is clear enough that Jdc 2 1-5 is a literary unit[183]. It is obviously to be separated from chapter 1 on account of style, and from 2 6ff. because of sharply differing subject matter. Within the piece, there are no signs of literary seams. Since ample evidence is lacking to decide surely whether or not v. 1. 5a preserve old sanctuary tradition[184], the option of seeing a Form I simplest report here is not a clear choice. Furthermore, it is difficult to view these five verses as a tightly constructed tradition unit, for the name etymology is subordinate, almost digressive, to the thrust of the weightiest part of the piece, namely the programmatic message delivered by the angel of Yahweh.

This passage displays some typical features of a Form II simple report. Verse 5a, which appears like the β element of Form I, is motivated directly by the event reported in v. 4b (note assonance). There is no γ element. The setting given in v. 1 specifies a locale and anticipates the name. The narrative material is not neutral. Not only is v. 1 related to the name, but v. 4a is formulated to express connections between the angel's speech and v. 4f. Yet the whole is not a simple Form II report, for the naming and its etymology does not come at the close of the material and the inferential function of v. 5a is not clear. Verse 5b contains a narrative element, likely original, which is not directly related to the name tradition. Moreover, the relation between the name through its motivation to the main material of the piece is weak. "Weeping" is a quite general reaction only loosely suggested by the actual reported content of the message. One might contrast the tightly knit logical relationships in Gen 32 2f. Num 11 1ff. Gen 38 27-30, for example.

All these considerations lead to the conclusion that at best, the etymological formula here expresses a subordinate motif in a larger

---

[183] Cf. the commentaries.
[184] Nowack, Richter, 13, suggests this possibility.

whole, and that it assumes a mixed form close to that of a Form II simple etiological report.

6. Jdc 15 17

This verse is part of a more or less homogenous literary block in chapters 14 and 15. There is no sign that v. 17 is a literary gloss[185]. Yet in the history of traditions, Gressmann has argued that the name tradition in v. 17 was of independent origin[186]. The new beginning in v. 17a tends to support this judgment, since such expressions in Judges generally introduce a new traditional piece[187]. Moreover, v. 17 lies somewhat outside the chapter's thematic development which clearly reaches its climax and resolution in v. 15[188]. The attachment of the tradition in v. 18-19 is surely secondary to the growth of these materials in their pre-literary stages. They have nothing except Samson and the locale in common with 15 1-16. 17.

In terms of criteria for etymological etiological report, it is clear that v. 17 itself is closest to a Form II simple report, even though its formulation is like that of Form I. Lacking a γ element, and being linked to the preceding verse, it reports an event which provides the direct motivation (17aβ) for the particular name reported in v. 17b. The name, as elsewhere, expresses a synonym to a verb used in the reported motivation[189]. Yet this name tradition is only loosely linked to specific narrative elements outside of v. 17. The name of the place is already assumed in v. 9 and 14; the noun "jawbone" appears in v. 15. There is nothing of the tight relationship characteristic of the Form II simple report in which the narrative elements drive toward the etymology. The name is not connected by assonance, or synonym, or commensurate descriptive response. At best it picks up a detail unimportant to the substance of the account of victory. In fact this very detail in v. 15, the story's resolution, may be related to the use of the poetic saying in v. 16 more than to the subsequent Form I of v. 17. Of course, there is no question of a developed report here, since the name is not motivated by the resolution in v. 15. It

---

[185] Cf. Moore, Judges, 345; Budde, Richter, 104; Gressmann, Anfänge, 240 ff. et al.

[186] Gressmann, Anfänge, 245 f.

[187] Richter, Untersuchungen, 358. Cf. 6 25 7 9 9 42. Cf. also the Dtr inserts in 6 7 and 8 33.

[188] The speech in v. 16 is probably of independent origin. Cf. Gressmann, Anfänge, 246. Also, Simpson, Composition, 60.

[189] Tradition probably understood רמת לחי from the verb רמה "to throw away." Even if originally this were not the sort of word play intended, the etymology is still within the realm of the typical because of the occurrence of לחי in the name and its particular motivation.

appears likely, therefore, that a mixed form appears in a simple report, and merely plays a subordinate role in its wider context.

7. Jdc 6 24

This verse falls at the close of a passage (v. 11-24) which presents major problems for analysis. It is clearly to be separated from the Dtr piece in 6 1-10[190] and v. 25-32 which deal with altogether different themes. Recently, W. Richter[191] has subjected this passage to rigorous and precise examination. He finds various doublets (e. g., 11a//11b. 11a//12a), alternation of messenger names (e. g., מלאך יהוה and מלאך האלהים), and other major thematic inconsistencies (e. g., v. 14. 16 contrast with v. 22-24; מנחה is merely food for a guest in v. 18 and an offering for a god in v. 20). Richter then lifts out two literary layers: v. 11a. 18-19. 21-24, and v. 11b-17. He postulates further that in the oral tradition, the earliest stage spoke of Gideon and a divine visitation; later, the first elements of the altar tradition (v. 22. 24) came in because Gideon was traditionally connected with an altar at Ophra; finally the grounding for the name (v. 23) was added[192]. Thus the report of naming was not originally connected with the preceding narrative complex (v. 11a. 18-19. 21) and the motivation for the particular name given to the altar belongs to a still younger layer of tradition. A key point made by Richter is that in tradition generally, theophany was schematically associated with altar building and naming (Gen 35 1. 3. 7 "E"; and Gen 12 7 13 14-18 26 24f. "J")[193] but not always with etymology (Gen 12 7 13 14-18 26 24f.). The question is open, then, whether or not in Jdc 6, even though it is a matter of epiphany more than theophany, the etymological interest reflects a secondary growth in the tradition.

Already v. 23, which presumably makes the etymological word play, is suspect because it breaks the schematic connection of theophany (v. 21f.) and altar building (24a). Moreover, the speech in v. 23 is attributed to Yahweh, a rather abrupt turn of affairs in the context of מלאך יהוה (v. 21. 22). Further, the thematic climax surely falls upon the recognition in v. 22. In this case the speech in the following verse is at least anti-climactic. Hence, there is some support for viewing the etymological elements as secondary accretion.

Corroboration is found in the application of our form critical criteria. As the text now stands, an etymological formula (v. 24aβ)

---

[190] Cf. Noth, Studien, 51.

[191] Untersuchungen 122 ff.

[192] Ibid. 128—144.

[193] In "J", the phrase ליהוה substitutes for the naming. Richter op. cit. 135. One should note that Gen 33 20 has altar building and naming, but no theophany!

receives its direct motivation in the Yahweh speech (v. 23)[194]. The link, however, between motivation and name is surprising, if not atypical. The transition from speech-motivation to name is accomplished neither by assonance, synonym, nor commensurate descriptive response. A word of greeting (שלום לך), in itself odd in the context of a conventional theophany speech, "Fear not . . ."[195], simply appears again as a part of the name. The step from one to the other is rough and obscures a direct causal relationship. One would have expected normally a name such as "Yahweh gives peace" or a motivation speech such as "I am peace to (for) you." In short, the name given does not reproduce the *substance* of the motivational speech, and hence represents a breakdown of the conventional pattern. One might even suppose with Richter[196] that the known altar name (without etymology) provided the occasion for the formulation of the greeting in Yahweh's mouth. Moreover, the conventional pattern of etymological report — mixed or otherwise — is not clearly visible here. Significantly, the motivation is separated from the name giving by what under normal circumstances would function as a setting in which the name might arise. In view of the evidence, it seems likely that a genuine etymological etiological report is not present. Rather, one sees the secondary accretion of etymological interests which are expressed in an oddly mixed form.

---

[194] Verse 24b clearly has nothing to do with etymology, since the permanence and location of the altar itself is attested. This is without doubt secondary to the narrative account. (Childs, JBL 82, 1963, 285f.)

[195] L. Köhler, Die Offenbarungsformel 'Fürchte dich nicht' im AT, SthZ 36 (1919), 33—39.

[196] Op. cit. 132.

Section II
Significative Etiology
PART A. '*ÔT* SCHEMA AS ETIOLOGY
I. '*Ôt Formulae*

The word '*ôt* (אוֹת), which occurs some seventy-nine times in the Old Testament, appears in a rather broad semantic range[1]. In the main, it refers to the following distinct objects:

(1) A prophetic sign-act, e. g. Ez 4 1-3.

(2) Event predicted by prophet as "sign", e. g. I Sam 10 1. 7. 9 Jes 38 7.

(3) Event predicted, but which consists of miraculous, extraordinary happenings, e. g. plagues and wonders in Egypt.

(4) Event not connected with prophets, but a miraculous deed performed by Yahweh alone, e. g. in theophany stories such as Jdc 6 11ff.

(5) Event in the heavens, e. g. Jer 10 2 and in Gen 9 12ff.

(6) A cultic practice or regulation, e. g. Gen 17 11.

(7) An event in the *Heilsgeschichte*, or an object which recalls the same, e. g. Jos 4 6.

An '*ôt* most commonly functions to engender knowledge (ידע or דעת); this function is occasionally differentiated to "sight" (e. g. Ps 86 17), "fear" (e. g. Ps 65 8ff.), "hearing" (e. g. Ex 4 8), or "belief" (e. g. Num 14 11). Very often, function is expressed in a subordinate clause (e. g. introduced by כי Ex 3 12, or אשר Jes 38 7, or שׁ in Jdc 6 17)[2].

Originally in Israel '*ôt* seems to have designated the oracle or sign of revelation through which Yahweh made himself known to his people. Thus God's revelation of will was represented in some objective event which, of course, had to be given an interpretation[3].

---

[1] For what follows, cf. C. A. Keller, Das Wort OTH als Offenbarungszeichen Gottes, 1946, 49ff. Cf. also Rengstorf in Theologisches Wörterbuch zum Neuen Testament, ed. G. Kittel, VII 1964, 207ff. Sometimes '*ôt* occurs parallel with *zikkarôn*. On this word, cf. now W. Schottroff, 'Gedenken' im Alten Orient und im Alten Testament, 1964, 299ff.   [2] Keller op. cit. 56ff.

[3] Ibid. 69ff. for what follows. Keller feels that the roots of usage lie in the world of mantic practices. (Cf. his 81f.) But cf. the doubts of W. Zimmerli in ThZ 5 (1949), 374ff. The Akkadian word *ittu(m)*, while not certainly cognate with Hebrew '*ôt*,

In prophecy, the revelation-sign was used in two ways — as an act to be interpreted and as a predicted and already interpreted event, which was most commonly a miraculous deed of God.

This revelation-sign took on a characteristic of permanence as it was taken over into the stories of the origins of cultic institutions. From this was derived Deuteronomy's metaphorical use as a "sign upon your hand" (Dtn 13 9. 16).

A special usage for *'ôt* was given in the traditions connected with Israel in Egypt. Even here, the word occurs mostly in Deuteronomistic layers as a symbol of the uniqueness of God, i. e., the revelation of his being and power shown in his love for his people and their election among the nations.

Finally, the "P" writers took up all these aspects. In working them into a theology of *Gnadenordnung*, *'ôt* became a "guarantee-sign." Yet the magical roots of the concept and usage are still visible in the independence of this sign, that is in its self-sustaining character (e. g. the rainbow). In this sense, an *'ôt* assures and actualizes God's gracious ordering of the cosmos, mankind, and holy people.

From a form critical point of view, the word *'ôt* obviously appears in a variety of expressions connected with various verbs (e. g. עשה; שלח)[4]; הרבה; בוא; נתן; שית; שים). Occasionally, *'ôt* governs a verb, e. g. Ex 8 19 I Sam 10 9) but most of the time it occurs in the predicate — often as the object of a transitive verb (e. g. Jes 66 19 Ps 135 9 Gen 4 15 Jdc 6 17). Depending upon the precise context, *'ôt* can be related to other parts of the predicate with a variety of prepositions. For example:

(1) Most frequently, the preposition is ל, with the person to whom the *'ôt* is given, or upon whom it is laid (e. g. Gen 4 15) or before whom it is visible (e. g. Ex 4 30 Jos 24 17).

(2) Next most often, the preposition is ב translated as "against" (e. g. Dtn 6 22) or "in", "among" (e. g. Dtn 34 11 Num 14 11). Closely related is the use of על in Jes 20 3 ("against") and Ps 105 27 ("among").

(3) Once, the preposition is מן in the expression מֵעָם יהוה (Jes 7 11).

More significant, however, are the various idiomatic expressions which are frequently attested.

(1) זֶה לְךָ הָאוֹת[5]

If one allows for minor variations of gender and number, this expression, a "sign announcement", appears eight times: Ex 3 12 I Sam

---

shows a similar semantic range, and plays a prominent role in divination. Cf. CAD VII, 306.

[4] This analysis moves beyond the fundamental work of Keller at this point.

[5] A similar expression זֹאת אוֹת appears only in Gen 9 12. 17 in the immediate context of a common formula הָיָה לְאוֹת. It is considered along with the latter.

2 34 14 10 II Reg 19 29 20 9 (= Jes 37 30 38 7) Jer 44 29. It always occurs in a speech consisting of three elements whose order can vary somewhat. There is the announcement that there is to be a sign; its meaning is given, along with identification of the event which is to be the sign. The speech is nearly always a divine message, given once as a Yahweh speech (Ex 3 12) and mostly as a prophetic oracle clearly marked as a word from God. There is only one exception. Jonathan speaks in I Sam 14 10. In all cases, the 'ôt is a specific natural or supernatural event, predicted to occur at a single point in time in the future[6].

(2) מה אות

This interrogative clause occurs two times: II Reg 20 8 and Jes 38 22. In the former, the question is focused on a specific object in a concrete situation, and directly elicits the prophetic oracle in v. 9f. Hence the general contextual features for the question are similar to those noticed with the "sign announcement". Because of textual difficulties[7], no conclusions can be drawn from Jes 38 22. As an interrogative formula, however, it is at least not inconsistent with the situation in which someone asked for a specific sign (cf. Jes 7 11).

(3) אות הוא[8]

This idiom is attested three times: Ez 4 3 Ex 31 13. 17. The expression always occurs as a part of a Yahweh speech which provides stipulations for future action. Ez 4 3 lies close to the many examples of prophets' sign-acts. The phrase designates as 'ôt a concrete action in a definite situation, limited by certain historical conditions. In sharp contrast, Ex 31 13. 17 deal with the Sabbath as a cultic institution and clearly reflect priestly theology. It is important to note that the formula here designates a specific object as a sign, and invests it with a quality of permanence which transcends the limits of specific time points. Moreover, as will become apparent, Ex 31 13.17 are separable from Ez 4 3 because of the former's affinities with another formula common in P tradition.

(4) לאות

This expression appears as a part of the predicate with קשר (Dtn 6 8 11 18), נתן (Jes 8 18), שים Ez 14 8) and שמר (Num 17 25). The

---

[6] In I Sam 14 10 two events are projected into the future as predicted possibilities, one of which is identified as 'ôt.

[7] The verse is fragmentary and out of a proper context. 1 Q Is[a] has it in the margin; cf. M. Burrows (ed.), The Dead Sea Scrolls of St. Mark's Monastery, I 1950, plate XXXII. The LXX implies Hebrew זה for MT מה.

[8] Jes 7 14 reads לכן יתן אדני הוא לכם אות. This is clearly different from the אות הוא nominal clause. The personal pronoun, masculine here, is used for emphasis. (GK[2] 135a, cf. note 1.)

preposition in all cases is best translated by English "as". This is
made clear by Num 17 25 where Yahweh speaks to Moses, "Put back
Aaron's rod before the testimony to be kept *as* a sign (לאות) *for* the
rebels (לבני מרי)". Always לאות appears in a speech — by Yahweh
(Num 17 25 Ez 14 18), by a prophet delivering a divine message
(Jes 8 18), or by Moses (Dtn 6 8 11 18). The object or event which
is designated sign is either specific and limited to one point in time
(i. e., in Num 17 25 and Jes 8 18) or vaguely defined and existent in
all times (as in Ez 14 8 Dtn 6 8 11 18)[9]. In no case is the *'ôt* given
both a quality of specificity and permanence.

(5) היה לאות

The idiom היה ל, fundamentally equivalent to English "become", nar-
rows in the case of היה לאות and a few other expressions, to the nuance
"serve as"[10]. In this sense one has not strayed far from the usage of
לאות described above. The phrase "serve as a sign" (allowing for
variation in number and tense) occurs rather frequently in a variety
of contexts, and only in relatively late texts:

    (a) P material: Gen 1 14 9 13 17 11 Num 17 3.
    (b) D or Dtr materials: Ex 12 13 13 9. 16 Dtn 28 46 Jos 4 6
        (היה אות).
    (c) Late prophetic material: Jes 19 20 55 13 Ez 20 12. 20[11].

In every case, the idiom appears as a part of a speech — by Yahweh
(Gen 1 14 9 13 17 11 Ex 12 13 Num 17 3 Ez 20 12. 20), by a prophet
(Jes 19 20 55 13), by Moses (Ex 13 9. 16 Dtn 28 46), or Joshua (Jos
4 6). The speeches are mostly prescriptive, but include as well, threat
(Dtn 28 46), accusation (Ez 20 12. 20), and salvation oracle (Jes 19 20
55 13). The meaning of *'ôt* in these passages is never a sign-act or a
predicted event. On the one hand, *'ôt* refers to a specific object limited
to a single point in time (Ex 12 13 Jes 19 20 Ez 20 12. 20); on the
other hand, an object only vaguely specified serves as a sign for all
time in Dtn 28 46 and Jes 55 13. A sign which is both specifically
identified and given a quality of permanence without regard for
points in time is prescribed in Gen 9 13 (rainbow), 17 11 (rite of cir-

---

[9] Ps 74 4 and Jes 20 3, where אות, without ל occurs, and English "as" must be
supplied to convey the meaning, certainly are similar. In both these passages *'ôt*
is something specific and is bound to one time point.

[10] On this understanding of the idiom, cf. C. H. Ratschow, Werden und Wirken: Eine
Untersuchung des Wortes *hajah* als Beitrag zur Wirklichkeitserfassung des Alten
Testaments, 1941, 9 ff.

[11] Ex 8 19, an earlier text where היה אות occurs, does not yield the sense "serve as
a sign". In any case, the citation is of doubtful value, since the LXX implies a
different Hebrew reading.

cumcision), Num 17 3 (altar plate), Ex 13 9. 16 (*maṣṣôt* rite; first born sacrifice), Jos 4 6 (twelve stones at Gilgal)[12].

It is a remarkable fact that of all the idiomatic phrases, and of the seventy-nine times which '*ôt* appears in the Old Testament, only Gen 9 13 17 11 Num 17 3 (היה לאות P material), and Ex 31 13. 17 (אות הוא P material), bring together conceptually a specific object designated as '*ôt* and the quality of timeless permanence[13]. Only these passages now pertain to etiology. Moreover, these few passages are structured according to a stereotype schema consisting of the following elements:

(1) Identification of an object or rite
(2) Designation as a '*ôt* (היה לאות or אות הוא)
(3) Meaning of the '*ôt* (what it symbolizes, memorializes, recalls)
Of all other seventy-one occurrences of the word, regardless of idiom, only two passages (Ex 12 13 and Num 17 25) show a similar pattern, and this without the accent of a timeless permanence. One is justified, then, in looking more closely at this P material, and in considering the passages in question to be examples of a special *genre* connected in some way with the expression of etiological interests.

II. '*Ôt* Schema as Significative Etiology

Gen 9 8-17 (P)[14] offers a Yahweh speech — within a minimal narrative framework (v. 8. 12a. 17a) — which announces the covenant and its recipients (v. 9f.), gives its content (v. 11), and pronounces its sign (v. 12-17). Thematically the unit certainly stands apart from v. 1-7 and the genealogy in v. 18ff. The speech itself is not smooth[15]. A covenant is given twice (v. 9 and 11), the "sign" is announced in v. 12 and 17, the rainbow mentioned two times (v. 13 and 14), God's remembering twice in v. 14 and 16. These doublets, according to von Rad, confirm the impression that the present text is a conflation of

---

[12] Gen 1 14 והיו לאותת must be classified as a special case. Not only is the plural used (elsewhere only singular היה לאות) but the meaning of '*ôt* is very restricted: "They shall serve as signs for the fixed time periods," or "Let them mark the fixed times". (Cf. Speiser, Genesis, 6.)

[13] This special characteristic is present also in Ex 13 9. 16 and Jos 4 6. But these occasions bring היה לאות into proximity with a separate form, the question-answer schema (Ex 13 14-15 Jos 4 6-7). Hence they will be discussed as a Mixed Form below in Part IV.

[14] The text is clear, and there are no significant LXX variants. Source critics unanimously assign the material to P (Gunkel, Genesis, 147; Speiser, Genesis, 57; von Rad, Genesis, 129).

[15] Cf. G. von Rad, Die Priesterschrift im Hexateuch, 1934, 1 ff.

two earlier recensions: v. 8. 11a. 13. 16f. (equals A), and 9f. 11b. 12. 14f. (equals B).

In verse 12 (recension B) the word *'ôt* appears in a lengthy nominal clause which is paralleled in v. 17 (recension A). The formulation (זאת אות־הברית) is attested only here. Since in both cases the clause in no way identifies the "sign", their function is subordinated in this context to v. 13a. They serve as introduction and conclusion, announcing that a sign of the *berît* is to be (has been, in v. 17) given to all future generations. A certain stress, however, falls on v. 13, as shown by the inverted word order. It is here, both in version A (v. 13. 16) and the combined recension (v. 13-16), that the idiom היה לאות occurs as part of the *'ôt* schema:

(1) x identified: v. 13a, "My bow I set in the cloud"
(2) x designated *'ôt*: v. 13b
(3) Meaning of x as *'ôt*: v. 16

The sign formula is most reasonably translated as a future tense, "and it (the bow) shall serve as a sign of the covenant ..."[16]. Theoretically, of course, one may read a simple *waw* and retain a past sense for the Qatal verb form[17]. In the context, however, this seems highly unlikely. The blessing given in v. 1b-7 seems clearly open toward the future (imperatives — v. 1b. 7 — and a series of Yiqtal verb forms — v. 2. 5). The phraseology in v. 11a (ולא יכרת כל־בשר עוד), and the temporal clause in v. 16a (both in recension A) certainly look toward a future time. The wider context, therefore, provides warrant for reading v. 13b as a future tense. The *'ôt* formula points toward a future which begins in the present because now the bow is set in the cloud.

Moreover, the *'ôt* itself is given a quality of permanence. The bow functions (v. 16) to recall the promise, i. e., the covenant, forever. This fact is confirmed even in the combined recension, for the "sign of the covenant" (v. 12) is established as existent for all subsequent points in time with the characteristically P phrase לדרת עולם[18]. From the viewpoint of the reader or hearer, therefore, something specific (the rainbow) as *'ôt* has existed from the past of Noah's time to the present of the hearer's generation, and will continue to exist in the future. The bow possesses an independent power before Yahweh and men to recall or memorialize for all time the promise given[19]. At

---

[16] So F. Blake, A Resurvey of Hebrew Tenses, 1951, prgr. 35 *l'*.

[17] Ibid. prgr. 37 *a'*.

[18] לדרתם or לדרתיכם in Gen 17 7. 9. 12 Ex 12 14. 17. 42 16 32. 33 Lev 3 17 6 11 7 36 Num 9 10 10 8 et al. (For a complete listing, cf. S. Driver, An Introduction to the Literature of the Old Testament, 1913², 132.)

[19] On a probable mythological background for this divine bow ("my bow" v. 13a), cf. Gunkel, Genesis, 151.

Yahweh's command, it serves as a memory sign, as a way of actual-
izing again and again the promise of v. 16[20]. In this context, then,
the '*ôt* schema serves primarily to provide the meaning of the rainbow. The form functions to present a *significative etiology*, that is,
an explanation of the "sign-ness" of the bow, what it recalls and
guarantees forever. Of course, in light of the wider context, particularly v. 11a and v. 1-7, one cannot overlook a certain broadening of
perspective within the whole priestly theology[21]. But in itself, one
can see the '*ôt* schema expressing and emphasizing the significance of
the bow for the ordering of Israel's existence.

Gen 17 9-14 offers another divine speech with only a minimal
narrative setting (v. 9a). Here God speaks to Abraham, commands
the observance of the covenant, and provides its content by prescrib-
ing circumcision. Clearly P material[22], the section is separated from
the surrounding traditions by the narrative formulae (v. 9a. 15a). It
surely has nothing to do with v. 15ff. which deal with a covenant
with Isaac. Yet v. 9-14 are not unified. On the one hand, v. 10-12a. 13b
are cast as a direct speech mostly in plural address style[23]. On the
other hand, v. 12b-13a specify detailed prescriptions in a singular address form. Moreover, v. 14 is impersonally cast in a style at least
reminiscent of a conventional type of legislation (cf. Ex 12 15. 19
31 14 Num 9 13 Lev 7 20f. 17 9 19 8 *et al.*)[24]. One might conclude
from this disarray, as does von Rad[25], that an earlier layer (v. 9-12a.
13b) has been secondarily expanded by the detailed prescriptions
(v. 12b-13a), and perhaps by v. 14[26].

If such an understanding be correct, then the sign formula, as
well as the entire '*ôt* schema is contained in the earlier tradition. The
elements:

---

[20] Only in relation to the wider context can one generalize at this point and speak
of the sign guaranteeing the "Gnadenordnung" (Keller op. cit. 132), or the "sta-
bility of nature" (von Rad, Genesis, 130).

[21] Keller op. cit. 130ff.

[22] Cf. commentators. E. g., Gunkel, Genesis, 264; Speiser, Genesis, 122.

[23] Only the minor זרעך אחריך disturbs this pattern.

[24] For a study of this formula, cf. W. Zimmerli, Die Eigenart der prophetischen Rede
des Ezechiel, ZAW 66 (1954), 13ff.

[25] Priesterschrift 22—24.

[26] The final form of v. 10b-13, however, shows a certain symmetry which may, after
all, turn out to be characteristic for much of redacted P legislation:

        A Stipulation: v. 10b-11a
        B It is a "sign of the *b[e]rît*": v. 11b
        A' Stipulation: v. 12-13a
        B' Covenant is "everlasting": v. 13b.

(1) X identified (circumcision prescribed): v. 10b-11a
(2) X designated '*ôt*: v. 11b[27]
(3) Meaning of X as '*ôt*

The '*ôt* formula should be read with conversive *waw* as future tense. The whole section is oriented toward the future — or at least general present — in the manner of legislation, and demands a certain openness to the future. The phrase זרעך אחריך (v. 10b) points to a similar conclusion.

The '*ôt* itself is given a quality of permanence without regard for specific points in time. Already the earlier tradition understood the sign, i. e., the rite of circumcision, to be applicable to the generations following Abraham (v. 10b). The later expansions were more explicit: v. 12a לדרתיכם; v. 13b לברית עולם. One sees, therefore, that the sign has existed from the past of Abraham into the present and indefinite future. The ritual act prescribed is the sign of God's covenant[28]. It recalls, memorializes, points to, the special relationship between God and Abraham; and it marks each participant as a bona fide descendant of Abraham[29]. Like Gen 9 13ff., the '*ôt* schema here presents a significative etiology. It expresses the "sign-ness" of a cultic rite certainly known and presupposed in the priestly theology (cf. Lev 12 3). Through its designation as sign of the covenant, circumcision is both commanded and explained as a meaningful memory sign in the ordering of God and people.

A similar situation is apparent in Num 17 1-5. Following the destruction of Korah and company, Moses receives a series of commands, each with its own motive clause. He is to take up the censers belonging to Korah's men, scatter the fire, and hammer the pots into an altar covering. The latter is to serve as a sign (v. 3), a reminder (*zikkarôn*) to the Israelites[30].

---

[27] Two MSS, S, and a MS of Targum read והיתה, presumably in agreement with the preceding ערלתכם. Perhaps, however, the feminine singular refers to the whole clause. Cf. GK² 144b.

[28] The third singular masculine והיה has as its antecedent the preceding clause (cf. GK² 144b).

[29] Cf. further on the theological significance, Keller op. cit. 135.

[30] There are several textual problems. (1) MT בנפשתם ... כיקדשו (v. 2-3a). As the Hebrew reads, a stative (קָדֵשׁ) governs an accusative. The Greek MSS mostly read ηγιασαν τα πυρεια των αμαρτωλων τουτων ... ψυχαις αυτων thus implying MT and probably reading the D stem קִדְּשׁוּ. A few versions, however, have ηγιασθησαν. A movement from the pure operation of stative verbs to that of an active verb is attested elsewhere (cf. GK² 117 note 2). Gray (Numbers 211) drops MT את and takes מחתות to be subject of קדשו. In any case the meaning is clear: the censers are now sanctified and therefore warrant the extraordinary commands given in v. 2. (2) For MT וְעָשׂוּ, read imperative וַעֲשֵׂה with some Greek

Commentators generally agree in assigning these five verses to a priestly redactor[31]. They are clearly independent of v. 6ff. There are no points of contact with the earlier material preserved in 16 12-15. 25-34. Therefore, on the level of tradition history, v. 1-5 were linked up only with the later form of the preceding Korah tradition. Yet even this connection is loose, as is shown in the rather forced linkage brought about in v. 5.

The piece is made up of narrative elements (v. 1 and 4), a Yahweh speech (v. 2f.), and a reflective comment (v. 5)[32]. The whole is organized loosely according to the '*ôt* schema:

(1) X is identified (making of altar plates prescribed): v. 2-3a
(2) X designated '*ôt*: v. 3b
(3) Meaning of X as '*ôt*: v. 5

The '*ôt* formula, as in Gen 9 and 17, is best translated with a future sense: "They shall serve as an '*ôt*," or "Let them serve as an '*ôt* ...". The pointing of the verb ויהי, in contrast to the immediately preceding narrative tense, indicates as much. Moreover, the general prescriptive character of the whole speech suggests a certain openness to the future.

More importantly, the sign has a significance which is not limited to a particular point in time. The '*ôt* formula itself expresses this characteristic. It is a sign to the "Israelites" — not those said to participate in the events of Korah's rebellion, for the phrase בני ישראל only occurs in 16 2 in a special bound phrase — but to those Israelites who live in future generations.

One has only to contrast the timebound significance of the "sign" in 17 25 where Aaron's blooming staff is to be an '*ôt* to the rebels (לבני מרי) that "you (Moses) may make an end to their murmurings ...". Here the fact and meaning of the sign is rooted in the preceding narrative of rebellion (17 16ff.). It has meaning only at this

---

MSS and Syriac. This is parallel, then, to the preceding אָמַר and זָרֶה. (3) MT ויהי (v. 3b); S reads והיו and the LXX reads a past tense (εγενοντο; a few read εγενετο). On the basis of parallel '*ôt* passages, a future sense in the '*ôt* formula is likely; also the resumption of a narrative tense at this point is awkward and abrupt. Therefore the Greek reading is not probable.

[31] E. g., Baentsch, Exodus, Leviticus, Numeri, 549f.; H. Holzinger, Numeri, 66; Gray, Numbers, 208.

[32] The breakdown of strict narrative style in v. 5 is seen in the generalized impersonal formulation of the למען אשר clause. Also, the phrase *b°yad mošæ* in Numbers never occurs in strict narrative. It is, rather, a redactional feature having no special narrative function. Cf. 33 1 (superscription) 9 23 27 23 36 13 4 37. 45. 49 (concluding formulae) 10 13 (digressive tabulation of facts) 15 23 (legal prescription).

specific point in time, i. e., to those particular rebels. Now in 17 3,
one begins to see that the very lack of specificity in the expression
ויהיו לאות לבני ישראל, points to an openness to an indefinite future
which gives permanent significance to the "sign", namely, the altar
covering. This understanding is confirmed in the wider *'ôt* schema
also. The "sign" stands parallel to *zikkarôn* of v. 5, which is to be a
reminder for generations after Aaron (מזרע אהרן). It is further corroborated by the clause beginning with למען אשר (v. 5), which is impersonally formulated to suggest its applicability, like legislation, in
every subsequent and similar situation.

Hence a specific object, the altar covering, has been given a
quality of permanence as a sign, as a reminder of Korah's fate, as
a mark of Aaron's special privilege before Yahweh's altar in all
generations. The *'ôt* schema in itself, therefore, functions as a significative etiology when it explains the "sign-ness" of an altar covering
which elsewhere is simply prescribed (Ex 27 1ff. 38 1ff.)[33].

The situation is more complex in Ex 31 12-17. In the context of
diverse cultic prescriptions linked together loosely by a minimal narrative framework (Ex 30 11. 17. 22. 34 31 1. 12. 18), Yahweh commands
the people through Moses to observe the Sabbath (v. 13a)[34]. There
follow in v. 13b-17 very complex traditions circling in various ways
about this fundamental theme.

Commentators generally agree that these verses stem from priestly redaction[35]. There are numerous points of tension. Verse 14a essentially repeats v. 13; v. 14b shows two conventional legal formulations,
each having a distinctive *Sitz im Leben* and history. On the one hand
there is מחלליה מות יומת[36]; on the other, something like a casuistic form

---

[33] W. Schottroff (Gedenken 317) echoes most commentators in judging Num 17 1-5
as a secondary piece with "etiological tendency".

[34] On the form of the command, cf. Lev 19 3. 30 26 2. The use of *wăyyomær* in this
introductory formula (v. 12) is rare in P material, where the usual expression employs
wăyᵉdăbber. Cf., for example, Ex 25 1 30 11. 17. 22 31 1 40 1 et al. But cf. Lev 16 2
21 1. The formula does not necessarily indicate a literary break in the material.
Cf. its use in Lev 22 26 in the midst of a single collection of law (Lev 22 17-30). Not
even the *waw* following לאמר (v. 13) signals a break. Such usage is common in
priestly formulations. Cf. Lev 16 2 20 1 Ex 30 17f. 22f. (the latter has ואתה). The
use of *'ăk* here in Ex 31 13 indicates that we are to read what follows in close relationship with the preceding regulations. (Cf. Lev 23 27. 39 27 26. 28.)

[35] Cf. Holzinger, Exodus, 147; Baentsch, Exodus-Lev-Num, 267ff.; Driver, Exodus,
344; Beer, Exodus, 151f.; Noth, Exodus, 241. Cf. also von Rad, Priesterschrift, 62ff.

[36] Cf. A. Alt, The Origins of Israelite Law, in his collection: Essays on Old Testament
History and Religion, 1966, 103ff.; the German original in: Kleine Schriften zur
Geschichte des Volkes Israel, I 1953. Recently, E. Gerstenberger, Wesen und Her-
kunft des 'apodiktischen Rechts', 1965.

כי העשה בה מלאכה ונכרתה[37]. Verses 15 ff. take up the theme again in what appears to be a secondary expansion[38]. But even here there is clumsiness of formulation; verses 15 and 17b refer to Yahweh in the third person and v. 17a appears to be spoken by Yahweh himself. Moreover, v. 16 begins again a Sabbath commandment following the self-contained law of v. 15. (Cf. Ex 35 2 Lev 23 3 et al.)

The complexity of the whole fabric undoubtedly stems partly from obscure developments in pre-literary history; literary analysis, therefore, is unable to resolve all the problems[39]. Fully aware of the difficulties, however, one can examine the '*ōt* material here simply because it appears to have been included in fairly distinct tradition stages, which still assert their independence within the whole complex.

Verse 13 stands out first. Following a command in second plural address, a *kî* motive clause identifies the Sabbath as an '*ōt* whose significance is given in the infinitival clause immediately following. The '*ōt* schema is operative here.

(1) X is identified (Sabbath prescribed)
(2) X is an '*ōt*
(3) Meaning of X as '*ōt*

The nominal clause '*ōt* formula, of course, is different from that in Gen 9 13 17 11 and Num 17 3. Yet its scope is comparable. It plays the expected role in the larger schematic structure, identifies a given specific object as a "sign", and within itself attests to the latter's permanence in all time (לדרתיכם).

A certain modification has taken place, however. The context indicates that כי אות הוא be read most naturally as a present tense. Insofar as the '*ōt* formula, then, functions as a present tense motive clause, it makes an appeal to a state of affairs already presupposed[40]. Thus strictly speaking, the '*ōt* formula does not *designate* the Sabbath as a sign, but cites its "sign-ness" as a reason for obeying the law. This slight modification comes about because the dominant interest here is in the prescription. The inverted word order את־שבתתי תשמרו, as well as the syntactical subordination of the '*ōt* formula, definitely point in this direction.

---

[37] Ibid. 112 note 74, where Alt speculates that the original text may have been closer to the pure apodictic formulation. In any case the tension between the two forms dealing with the same subject in the same verse is unmistakable. On casuistic law in general, cf. ibid. 88 ff.

[38] Cf. Noth, Exodus, 204 f.

[39] Compare the commentators' attempts, and von Rad, Priesterschrift, 62 ff.

[40] Cf. B. Gemser, Motive Clauses in the Old Testament, Suppl. VT, I (1953), 50 ff. On the various kinds of appeals, classified according to content, cf. 55 ff.

In view of this shift in functions, one cannot speak simply of an *'ôt* schema presenting a significative etiology in v. 13. Insofar as the command in its formulation attests to the "sign-ness" of the Sabbath as a specific reality for all time, the special etiological interests are expressed. But the movement away from simply presenting an observance or object along with its "sign-ness", as in Gen 9 and 17 and Num 17, must be recognized. Perhaps even a certain deterioration in the form is visible in this functional shift.

Verses 16f. (*'ôt* in v. 17a), only thematically connected to what precedes, present a different picture. Short of postulating v. 17a to be a literary gloss, for which good evidence is lacking, there seems to be no way of resolving the tensions in the text between an impersonal third person style (v. 16. 17b) and a first person speech (v. 17a)[41]. But on the level of the final redaction of the text, there is good reason for taking v. 16f. as a unified Yahweh speech.

(1) The occurrence of בני ישראל in both v. 16 and 17 reflects a common stance with regard to the hearer of the command. In v. 16 it is possible to understand ושמרו as an indirect imperative: "And let the Israelites keep the Sabbath . . .". There is no grammatical awkwardness in this construction, even in direct address. Cf. Gen 41 33f., for example.

(2) It is not impossible that the speaker (Yahweh) slips easily back and forth between direct address in the second person, third person indirect address, or impersonally formulated legal prescription. A case in point is Lev 22 3. Here is found a Yahweh speech to Moses with the second person address suffixes (לדרתיכם; מכל זרעכם), an impersonally formulated bit of legislation (כל איש אשר־יקרב), and references to the speaker (Yahweh) in both third and first persons (ליהוה; אני יהוה; מלפני)[42]. All this probably points to heavy editing[43]. Yet clearly v. 3 is to be understood in its final mixed form as a unified piece of legislation. This sort of clumsy formulation is by no means rare in priestly material, especially in tradition blocks bearing the marks of old legal material having been reworked for a later age. (Cf. Lev 17 12-16 21 16-23 23 28-30.) One is not surprised, therefore, to find in the case of Ex 31 16-17 similar fluctuations. Since it is clearly a question of material edited by priestly writers, the fluctuations do

---

[41] I take v. 15 to be a self-contained unit, originally independent of v. 13ff. and 16ff. Cf. above, 74f.

[42] LXX presupposes Hebrew אלהיכם, second plural address.

[43] Cf. R. Kilian, Literarkritische und formgeschichtliche Untersuchung des Heiligkeitsgesetzes, 1963, 92. Also H. Reventlow, Das Heiligkeitsgesetz, 1961, 97ff. Cf. however, K. Elliger, Leviticus, 1966, 285, who explains the fluctuation in style by a late author's familiarity and dependence upon customary formulae.

not count decisively against understanding the two verses as a redactional unit[44].

(3) The asyndetic beginning of v. 17 requires the context supplied by v. 16.

We therefore are justified in considering v. 16-17 at least in its final form, as a unified Yahweh speech. As such, the verses assume a pattern which is regularly found in priestly legal materials: a law is prescribed, and is followed immediately by a reflective comment — not a motive clause — often expressed by a nominal clause. (Cf. Num 18 23 Ex 27 21 28 43 et al.) Now the 'ôt formula in v. 17a is a part of the reflective comment, and at the same time functions in the 'ôt schema:

(1) X identified: v. 16 (Sabbath prescribed)
(2) X is an 'ôt: v. 17a
(3) Meaning of X as 'ôt: v. 17b

As in v. 13, the 'ôt formula, while formally distinct, functions similarly to the היה לאות form of Gen 9. 17 and Num 17. Its position in the larger schematic structure as well as its marking a specific object as a sign for all times, confirms this judgment. Already v. 16 has specified the permanence of the Sabbath and its observance[45]. One should note, however, the possibility that the 'ôt formula stands closer to a legal motive clause, as did v. 13, than do the examples of היה לאות. There is ambiguity in the nominal clause insofar as it can be read as a statement of a presupposed or known situation rather than merely a *designation* of Sabbath as 'ôt. Again, the beginnings of a breakdown in a conventional 'ôt formula are perhaps visible.

The sign is not a mark of Israel's holiness as was the case in v. 13. Rather its significance as sign lies in its recalling the majestic fabric of Gen 1—2 4a, or more specifically, the six days of creation work, and the seventh day of rest (cf. Ex 20 11 Gen 2 3). A vestige of an etymological word play may remain in the assonance of שָׁבַת and שַׁבָּת (cf. Gen 2 2). Accordingly we must not overlook a certain interest in the origin of the Sabbath and its name. Yet the formulation chiefly presents the demand for observance, and the "sign-ness" of the Sabbath. To this extent, the 'ôt schema of v. 16f. functions as significative etiology; it explains the Sabbath as a commanded reality,

---

[44] Cf. further Ex 24 1. 2 and Gen 9 16, both Yahweh speeches in which the speaker refers to himself in the third person. In poetry, of course, the stylistic feature is well known. Cf. for example, Hi 40 2. 9. 19 Jes 49 7 51 3. In Ugaritic, cf. texts 51:III:15ff.; 51:IV:36ff.; 76:II:20ff.; 77:18. Cf. C. Torrey in JAOS 57 (1937), 405ff., and S. Gewirtz in VT 11 (1961), 147 note 4.

[45] Verse 16 stresses the observance which is to be an ordinance forever (taking *bᵉrît* in its derived sense of "law" or "ordinance". Cf. Lev 24 8 and Keller, OTH, 141).

and its meaning as a memory sign recalling Yahweh's creative acts
in ordering the primeval cosmos.

To summarize: a formula היה לאות is used in P materials to designate a specific object or cultic rite as a sign which recalls perma-
nently something of specified content and import in the priestly view
of God's ordering of the world. The formula, read as a future tense,
occurs always in the midst of a fixed structure which functions as a
whole to provide a significative etiology, that is, the meaning for all
time of a specific and already known act or object[46]. The deterioration
of this etiological form was observed in Ex 31 13. 17 where the formula
appears as a nominal clause (אות הוא), which tended to presuppose
rather than divulge or designate the "signship" of a given object.

PART B. THE QUESTION-ANSWER SCHEMA AS ETIOLOGY

J. A. Soggin has isolated five occasions, all of which are related
to cultic matters, on which children ask their fathers about the origins of a cultic practice or a sanctuary with peculiar features: Ex
12 26ff. 13 14ff. Dtn 6 20ff. Jos 4 6ff. 21ff. In a few other passages such
occasions are probably implicit: Dtn 4 10ff. 6 7ff. 11 19ff.[47]. The question-answer schema is reproduced with remarkable rigidity. Soggin
understands all the contexts variously as etiological. In Dtn 6 20ff.
the "credo" serves as the etiology of the observance of law; Ex
12 24-27 and 13 11-16 presuppose a cultic frame of reference, and must
therefore be understood etiologically; in Jos 4 6ff. 21ff., it is a question
of an etiology of the sanctuary at Gilgal, in which twelve stones
certainly played a role. Their presence is explained with an etiological
saga[48]. Because of their peculiarly specialized character, Soggin supposes that these five passages preserve fragments of an old catechism
wherein question and answer were asked and given liturgically. In
such a way, elemental instruction into important matters of the
Israelite cult was accomplished[49].

Disregarding for the moment those two occurrences which lie in
proximity to the word 'ôt (i. e. Jos 4 6f. and Ex 13 14-16), this question-
answer schema always appears as a conditional sentence. A protasis

---

[46] Num 15 37-40 is very similar to this 'ôt form, but contains neither the word 'ôt, nor
a synonym.

[47] J. A. Soggin, Kultätiologische Sagen und Katechese im Hexateuch, VT 10 (1960),
341—347. Cf. also L. Köhler, Hebrew Man (ET of German 1953 edition), 79f. Cf.
further, Dtn 32 7.

[48] Soggin op. cit. 342 ff.

[49] Ibid. 344 ff.

(temporal clause) contains the question which the children are to ask, and the apodosis prescribes the appropriate answer[50]. A typical full form occurs in Ex 12 26:

(1) והיה כי יאמרו אליכם בניכם
מה העבדה הזאת לכם
(2) ואמרתם

(then follows the answer)

There are, of course, minor variations in the protasis. The temporal expression כי והיה is replaced by אשר in Jos 4 21[51], and is shortened to כי in Dtn 6 20[52]; the *yiqtal* verb is שאל in Jos 4 21 and Dtn 6 20; both of these passages in addition show an adverbial מחר which opens the prescription to the indefinite future; often לאמר introduces the quotation. The question itself is always in the form of a nominal clause, introduced by the interrogative מה, and sometimes containing the dative expression לכם (Ex 12 26)[53]. As judged from the variety of interests expressed in the prescribed answer, the exact sense of the question is ambiguous, extending over and including nuances as "why so and so?", "what does so and so mean?", "what is so and so?"

The prescribed answer (apodosis) always begins with a simple *waw* and Qatal verb form (ואמרתם or ואמרת; once והודעתם in Jos 4 22). There follows another quotation — the answer — given as a recitation in the style of a "credo", e. g. Dtn 6 21ff.[54] Ex 12 27 Jos 4 22b. The items recited are various, and demand closer study.

In Ex 12 27a[55], the quoted recitation provides an explanation for the name of the Passover rite in a way reminiscent of the etymological

---

[50] A search for parallels to the cases cited by Soggin yielded nothing. Jos 22 24 (noted by Soggin) and Gen 32 17f. show at most that a similar formal structure can be used in quite dissimilar circumstances. Occurrences of interrogative idioms show a diversity of usage, but nothing parallel to Soggin's "catechetical" question. Cf., for example, the uses of מה־זה, מה זאת, מה ל and ל (noun) מה. The latter idiom appears in two of Soggin's passages: Ex 12 26 and Jos 4 6. Its nuance here seems to be "what does so and so *mean* to you?" Cf. Ez 37 18, and probably II Sam 16 2 Ez 12 22 Joel 4 4. It is significant, however, that an inquiry into the meaning or interpretation of something can be expressed by a nominal clause without the preposition ל, e. g., the late vision formulae: Sach 1 9 4 4 6 4 or Gen 21 29. In any case, no parallels for Soggin's five cases are attested.

[51] Cf. GK² 164d.   [52] Some versions read והיה however.

[53] Even the lengthy expression in Dtn 6 20b fits the pattern, since the 'ašær clause is subordinate to the main nominal clause.

[54] Cf. G. von Rad, The Form-Critical Problem of the Hexateuch, in The Problem of the Hexateuch and Other Essays, 1966, 1ff.

[55] Verse 27b resumes the third person narrative, and thus is not a part of the prescriptive question-answer schema.

etiological report. An assonantal word play provides the causal link between the named observance (זֶבַח־פֶּסַח) and an act of Yahweh in the past (פָּסַח). But also, the Passover rite recalls for all generations (v. 24) that complex of traditions which describe the last evening in Egypt, and which are capsulated in the recited answer of v. 27. Thus the question-answer schema functions etiologically: it provides the explanation of name and origin of a cultic observance. But also, it functions as a significative etiology insofar as it summarizes the essential tradition facts which the rite recalls and memorializes. The form of the question, "what does this service *mean* to you?" already points in this direction.

Similarly in Jos 4 22b[56] the prescribed answer summarizes the tradition events with which twelve stones were associated. As such, the recitation neither identifies the stones nor explains their origin. Rather it capsulates that which the stones memorialize, and to this extent explains them as a memory sign. This seems clear even though the word '*ôt* does not appear in the text. Hence, the question-answer schema (v. 21-22), in addition to providing for instruction, functions in a significative way, and brings one close to the operation of the '*ôt* form as a significative etiology. The final redaction, of course, shifts ground, and has these twelve stones engendering knowledge and reverence analogously to '*ôt* in, for example, Dtn 4 35.

The picture is somewhat more diffuse in Dtn 6 21-25. The prescribed answer recites the essential points in Israel's *Heilsgeschichte* (slavery, exodus, and receipt of the land), and the giving of law (חֻקִּים)[57]. But the homiletical interest so characteristic of Deuteronomy in general is vividly expressed not only by the context in which the question-answer schema is placed (v. 1-19), but by the final statements in the quoted answer (v. 24b-25) which seek to induce obedience, which in turn is "righteousness". In view of the diversity of elements within the answer, the children's question cannot simply ask for the origin of law, or its contents, or its meaning as some sort of memory-sign recalling Yahweh's past saving acts. One must say, rather, that in broad terms, the questioner seeks the significance of the divine statutes[58]. But the prescribed answer moves beyond interests in origin and those events which law recalls, to inculcating obedience.

---

[56] The rough transition to v. 23, as well as the change to second plural address style (although the Greek MSS are more harmonious with v. 22b in this respect) indicate that v. 23f. did not originally belong in this question-answer schema. (Cf. Noth, Josua, 39.)

[57] There is little evidence for restricting the scope of חֻקִּים here. It likely refers to the totality of Israel's legal traditions, and thus to the entire phrase of v. 20b. Cf. N. Lohfink, Das Hauptgebot, 1965, 54f.

[58] Cf. von Rad, Deuteronomy (ET of German first edition), 65.

Only in this special sense — unparalleled elsewhere — can one say that the question-answer schema functions in a significative way. The undeniable etiological elements are focused, therefore, on quite a specific goal.

In summary, the function of the question-answer schema is nuanced to a fair degree. Yet the three cases examined each provide for instruction of future generations and prescribe the significance of a special object — twelve stones at Gilgal, Passover rite, Law. Two of the three passages (Ex 12 24-26 Jos 4 21f.) clearly functioned to define that which the object in question recalled or memorialized for future generations. In the third case (Dtn 6 20ff.), the blurring of focus on this particular concern is likely due to Deuteronomy's dominant homiletical style and interest. One sees, therefore, that the question-answer structure has a function very similar to that of the *'ôt* schema previously identified as a significative etiology.

This judgment is confirmed by two striking instances in which the two schemata merge: Ex 13 11-16 and Jos 4 6f.

1. Ex 13 1-16

Commentators have generally agreed that Ex 13 1-16 is a composite section comprised of at least three distinct parts: v. 1-2; v. 3-10; v. 11-16. The disagreement came in how one describes precisely their origins — as R[D] and P (v. 1-2)[59], or Deuteronomistic type material with later addition in v. 1-2[60], or proto-Deuteronomy tradition[61].

Now within the complex v. 11-16, and following a common legal formulation[62], the question-answer schema appears (v. 14-15). It is certainly to be understood as a continuation of v. 11-13. The elements of the schema are typical. The prescribed answer to the children's question recites the essential tradition facts which explain both the origin and reason for a particular sacrificial practice simply prescribed in an older text (Ex 22 28f.). The formulation makes clear that the sacrifice of Israel's first born is in commemoration of Yahweh's deed in Egypt. In this sense, as in the pure examples of question-answer schemata, one has come near the *'ôt* significative etiology which provides the meaning of an object as memory sign.

---

[59] So the older commentators, e. g. Baentsch, Exodus, Leviticus, Numeri, 108f., and Beer, Exodus, 71f.

[60] So Noth, Pentateuch, 32 note 106.

[61] So N. Lohfink, Hauptgebot, 116ff. Chr. Brekelmans has rightly called for more precision in the terminology of such materials, and to this end sets out several criteria. Cf. his Die sogenannten deuteronomischen Elemente in Gen.-Num., Suppl. VT, XV (1965), 90—96.

[62] Cf. Lohfink op. cit. 113ff.

Indeed, an *'ôt* formula appears as the final statement in the prescribed answer (v. 16):

והיה לאות על־ידכה

The formula is set in the midst of a larger *'ôt* schema which now surrounds the question-answer form as a framework:

(1) X identified (first-born sacrifice prescribed): v. 11-13
(2) X is an *'ôt*: v. 16a
(3) Meaning of X as *'ôt*: v. 16b

Here, of course, it is not a question of a sacrificial practice being designated a real symbol in the sense that circumcision can be a "sign" (Gen 17 11). The localization of the *'ôt* "on your hand" (parallel to *ṭôṭapôt* "between your eyes") suggests that the whole formula is to be understood metaphorically[63]. Yet its import is certainly what one would expect. First born sacrifice as *'ôt* points beyond itself to a significance given by the following *kî* clause. The sacrifice recalls or memorializes the exodus (v. 16b). In itself, therefore, the *'ôt* schema functions typically to provide a significative etiology, insofar as it explains the "sign-ness" of a particular sacrificial practice.

The remarkable fact is that in combination, the form of neither the *'ôt* nor the question-answer schemata has been significantly altered. Moreover, each form retains its individual function. This very lack of alteration indicates that both forms have one function in common, namely significative etiology. This is simply reinforced in the merger.

The situation in v. 3-10 is similar, but less clear. Reminiscent of v. 16, an *'ôt* formula appears in v. 9 in the midst of prescriptive legislation structured somewhat loosely according to the *'ôt* schema:

(1) X identified (observance prescribed): v. 5-7
(2) X is an *'ôt*: v. 9[64]

והיה לך לאות על־ידך

(3) Meaning of X as *'ôt*: v. 9b

As with v. 16, the *'ôt* formula is to be taken as a metaphor. It remains clear, however, that the *maṣṣôt* observance is understood as a memory sign (אות // זכרון) which recalls Yahweh's act of deliverance from Egypt. The *'ôt* schema therefore typically functions to order an

---

[63] Cf. Noth, Exodus, 101f. The probability that *ṭôṭapôt* is a technical term for an ancient practice involving specific objects (perhaps beads), also forces one to see a metaphorical usage here.

[64] For MT והיה S reads והיו. Even if it expressed an indefinite subject, a plural has no clear referent in the context.

observance and to establish and explain its "sign-ness" for all time
(v. 10 מימים ימימה).

It is significant that the schema is broken by v. 8, a provision
for instruction of future generations: "And you shall tell your son
on that day, 'Because of this (which) Yahweh did for me when I
came out of Egypt'"[65]. The similarity to the quoted reply in the
question-answer schema is obvious and allows one to suppose that a
fragment of such remains in the text at this point. The parallel in
structure between v. 5-10 and 11-16, and the clear question-answer
form within the latter, points to the same conclusion[66]. If this be
correct, then one sees immediately that the *'ôt* schema has not been
significantly altered in combination with elements of a question-
answer form.

2. Jos 4 6-7

Chapters 3 and 4 present an unusually complex literary picture
which has defied satisfactory solution. The supposition of a plurality
of independent narrative strata here, whether identified with Penta-
teuchal sources[67], or "versions"[68], has not led to illuminating results.
Because the middlepoint of the whole, the "disappearance" of the
Jordan waters, is clearly enough reported only once, Noth[69] supposes
that one basic tradition of the crossing has been elaborated by many
hands. Accordingly, Noth identifies in chapter 4, v. 1b-2, most of v. 3,
most of v. 8-10, v. 13. 18b. 19-21a. 23 as the original layer of tradition
which explained twelve stones in terms of the Jordan crossing. In
his view, v. 4f. reflect younger tradition, and v. 6-7 younger still.

Whether or not one accepts Noth's understanding (and I am
convinced of its general correctness), it is clear that v. 4-7 interrupt
the smooth transition from v. 3 to 8. The command issued by Joshua
in v. 5 lacks the crucial element prescribed in v. 3, namely taking
the stones to the lodging place. Moreover, the expansive instructions
in v. 4ff. are much too broad to be included in the purview of v. 8a.
Therefore, v. 4-7 are rightly understood at least as an independent
layer, and perhaps as a literary addition to older tradition.

Following a brief narrative statement (v. 4-5a), Joshua commands
the selection of twelve stones "that this may be an *'ôt*." The typical

---

[65] The text may be corrupt, as בעבור זה is very unusual.

[66] Cf. N. Lohfink, Hauptgebot, 116 note 9.

[67] E. g., Gressmann, Anfänge, 130 ff., and recently, O. Eissfeldt, The Old Testament:
An Introduction (ET of German third edition, 1964, 248 ff.).

[68] E. g., Möhlenbrink, Die Landnahmesagen des Buches Josua, ZAW 15 (1938), 254 ff.,
and J. Dus, Die Analyse zweier Ladeerzählungen des Josuabuches (Jos 3—4 und
6), ZAW 72 (1960), 107—134; also, P. Saydon, The Crossing of the Jordan, CBQ
12 (1950), 194—207, and E. Vogt, Die Erzählung vom Jordanübergang, Biblica 46
(1965), 125—148.   [69] Josua 31 ff.

question-answer schema follows, and prescribes the stones' meaning which is to be taught future generations[70]. The focus is clearly on the stones as a memorial forever ("and these stones shall [let these stones] be a *zikkarôn* forever")[71]. To this end, the tradition fact which the stones recall, namely that the waters were cut off before the ark on its passage over the Jordan, is recited. The question-answer form, therefore retains its conventional function of explaining the permanent "sign-ness" of a specific object. Again one sees the similarity with the function of the *'ôt* schema significative etiology.

Although the word *'ôt* appears in this passage, and indeed parallel to *zikkarôn* in a portion of the question-answer schema, the conventional *'ôt* structure is not obvious. Yet the main outlines are clear enough to allow the supposition that the force of the form is still being exerted in the tradition. The twelve stones are to be an *'ôt* whose significance as "sign" is given by the question-answer schema. It is important to note that the latter not only remains unaltered by its proximity with *'ôt* motifs, but smoothly assumes an important role in providing the meaning of a "sign". The whole piece in addition to providing for instruction of the young, certainly functions similarly to an *'ôt* significative etiology.

Thus, the various degrees of combined forms — *'ôt* schema and a fragment of an answer (Ex 13 5-10), question-answer schema and a loose *'ôt* structure (Jos 4 6f.), *'ôt* and question-answer schema combined intact (Ex 13 11-16) — show the ease with which two formally distinct structures can merge. The lack of significant alteration upon merger confirms the conclusion that the schemata possess a mutual function, namely to provide a significative etiology. One should note the fact that the pure question-answer schemata as well as the mixed forms, appear only in Deuteronomy or Deuteronomy type material[72].

---

[70] The appearance of אשר at the beginning of the answer (v. 7) does not significantly alter the form. It is still a matter of stipulating an answer which is to be recited in response to a question.

[71] The precise translation of והיו . . . לזכרון, of course, is uncertain. I favor reading a conversive *waw* since עד־עולם elsewhere never appears in historical narration, and is always oriented toward the future in petition, promise, command, threat, homily, etc. Occasionally such speeches can be referred to as past events (e. g. I Sam 2 30 I Chr 15 2 17 12. 14. 22 23 13 Jer 35 6), but in themselves the speech is always open to the future. A clear indication of this orientation is given in the common phrase מעתה ועד־עולם, e. g. Jes 9 6 59 21 Ps 113 2.

[72] No real parallels in the ancient near eastern literature are known to me. A sampling of ritual texts yielded nothing. Cf. Pritchard, ANET², 325—358; also E. Reiner, Šurpu: A Collection of Sumerian and Akkadian Incantations, 1958. Nor do the northwest Semitic inscriptions, including the Ugaritic texts, show a prescriptive question-answer schema. The device of citing a question and its answer is, of course, characteristic of wisdom materials in the Old Testament (cf., for example, Prov

PART C. SIGNIFICATIVE ETIOLOGICAL NARRATIVE

The one remaining task is to see how the *'ôt* and question-answer schemata are related, on the primary level of tradition, to a wider narrative context. The form critical study has already pointed to a conclusion, for neither form shows a necessary functional link with narrative material. Both types occur only in a speech, and in no way require a "story" for their integrity and significance.

This conclusion is immediately obvious with respect to the question-answer schema in Dtn 6 20-25. Not only does the form function independently of its immediate context as a prescriptive speech, but the relational lines to a wider context cannot possibly be drawn to narrative. This is so in a general sense because the prologue of Deuteronomy is cast entirely as a Moses speech, and specifically because chapter 6 contains no genuine narration. By definition, then, the question-answer schemata are independent of a "story" context. The mixed form in Ex 13 11-16, since it stands as an independent pericope, in no way contradicts this conclusion[73].

The fact is borne out equally well in Ex 24 24-27a. This passage conforms to the schematic pattern, and predictably shows signs of being secondarily placed in the wider context. Verses 21-23. 27b belong to J[74] yet share no stylistic features with v. 24-27a. It is difficult to avoid the conclusion that the latter originally had nothing to do with the J account of Passover.

Similarly, Jos 4 21f. forms a self-contained unit which gives some indication of having been secondarily brought to its present location. It is set off from v. 23f. by the roughness of transition from v. 22 to v. 23; the shift to second person address in the latter sharply con-

---

23 29f. 29 20 Hi 28 12ff.). In this context belongs such rhetorical usages exemplified in the "Dialogue of Pessimism" (W. G. Lambert, Babylonian Wisdom Literature, 1960, text 6, lines 79 ff.) :

"What, then, is good ?"
"To have my neck and your neck broken,
And to be thrown into the river is good."

Probably the Egyptian speech of Atum, along with explanatory glosses, dating from the second millenium version of the Book of the Dead, belongs in this "wisdom" use of rhetorical question and answer (cf. Pritchard, ANET[2], 1f.). A similar rhetorical device appears often in Akkadian letters from various periods, but clearly shows no relation to the Old Testament significative etiology. Cf. for example, R. Pfeiffer, State Letters of Assyria, 1935, numbers 234 and 266.

[73] If a genuine mixed form is present in Ex 13 3-10, the conclusion is borne out here also, since this section is likewise independent of the context.

[74] The commentators are virtually in unanimous agreement on this point. Cf. for example, Baentsch, Exodus-Lev-Num, 100f. (who gives many stylistic keys to the identification); Beer, Exodus, 62ff.; Noth, Exodus, 97f.; cf. also Lohfink, Hauptgebot, 121 ff.

trasts with the recitative style of v. 22. Whether or not v. 21f. are
secondarily joined to the preceding tradition is debatable; critics are
divided because the evidence is not decisive. However, the preceding
narrative in all its complex stages of growth reports the origin of
twelve stones, and v. 21f. go their own thematic way in dwelling on
the stones' significance. Moreover, the question-answer schema was
clearly inserted into Ex 12, stood alone in Dtn 6 (also Ex 13 11-16),
and in a mixed formulation was shown to be secondary expansion in
Jos 4 1-8[75]. It seems likely, therefore, that the linkage to the material
in the latter parts of Jos 4 is likewise secondary.

Similarly, the study of the *'ôt* schema revealed no narrative elements constitutive of the form. Where they were present, they represented only a minimal framework which in no way shaped the
'ôt structure (Gen 9 8-17 17 9-14 and the somewhat deteriorated form
in Ex 31 12-17). Where narrative elements assumed more importance
(Num 17 1-5), the pure *'ôt* schema was broken insofar as a short narration reports the creation of a sign and its meaning.

In any case, the *'ôt* form never appears integrally related to
developed narrative materials. The schema occurs in a Yahweh
speech in Gen 9 distinctly unrelated to the earlier versions of the
flood account, and only loosely tied as epilogue to the priestly story.
In Gen 17, whereas v. 1-8 and 9-14, which contain the *'ôt* schema,
likely belong in one literary stratum[76], the immediate context for the
'ôt form is speech rather than narrative. In fact, the entire chapter
is characterized by its lack of developed narrative features. The same
is true of Ex 31 12-17, which provides the *'ôt* schemata with only a
minimal narrative framework characteristic of this entire section of
P legislation (Ex 25—31). Finally, Num 17 1-5 is very loosely related
to the traditions given in Num 16. There are no real ties to the older
layers still visible (i. e., 16 12-15, parts of v. 25-34), and only loose
connections to the P stratum now dominant in the final text form[77].
Indeed the latter reaches its dramatic climax in 16 35 where Yahweh's
wrathful fire settles the dispute forming the core of the tradition. At
best, the *'ôt* schema in Num 17 sounds a subordinate motif in the
whole complex.

It is clear, then, that neither the *'ôt* schema, nor the question-
answer form is integrally related to narrative. They, rather, stand
alone as speech, epilogue, or secondary expansion on older material.
Each form, as shown above, functions to transmit a significative
etiology. But neither can be used as a mark of etiological narrative.

---

[75] Cf. above 83 f.
[76] So von Rad, Priesterschrift, 20 ff.
[77] Most commentators assign Num 17 1-5 to a P redactor. Cf. for example, Baentsch,
Exodus-Lev-Num, 549; Holzinger, Numeri, 69; Gray, Numbers, 208.

Section III
Conclusions and Implications

As described in the introduction, the task of this investigation was to define in controlled circumstances certain repetitive features, motifs, or formulae as marks of narrative material whose main function was etiological.

With regard to the etymological materials, two distinct forms expressive of etiological interests were found to be operative. Form I was structured so as to report a naming (always with ויקרא or ותקרא), a name, and its reason (making a word play on the name). This form showed no functional connections with narrative material surrounding it, and hence could not serve as a mark of etymological etiological narrative.

A second form was characterized by a reported event from which an inference to a name was drawn (by means of an על־כן conclusive clause, and often completing a word play). This Form II was a feature of etymological etiological narrative. Indeed, the essential structure remained unaltered in brief reports of varying complexity, and in two relatively developed narratives (Gen 11 1-9 26 23-33). In both latter cases, the inference was drawn from an indispensable element in the dramatic movement; that is, the name was based on the resolution of a tension present at the beginning of the narrative.

It is important to note that in no case was the etymological interest a focal point for extensive narrative tradition. The two most complex occurrences of Form II were in stories only anecdotal in length; of the many passages sharing characteristics of both Form I and II, the two most highly developed clearly showed the etymologies to be subordinate to other narrative interests. Most of the time, etymological etiology was expressed by a formula (Form I) or short report (Form II and Mixed Forms) in secondary or at least subordinate layers of tradition. Therefore, as marks of etiological narrative, the etymological forms offer little. It seems likely that in Israel, the etymological interest was not a real force in the building of extensive narrative material.

The 'ôt schema and the question-answer form were also discussed as etiological motifs. Both of these forms explained the origin and "sign-ness", i. e., significance in Israel's common life, of certain phenomena or customs. Yet both forms stood alone as speech, epilogue, or secondary expansion on older material. Neither form showed a constitutive link to narrative traditions, and thus could not serve as a mark of etiological narrative. The interest in preserving and transmitting certain known phenomena as memory signs apparently lacked the power to give rise to extensive narrative material.

The results of this investigation parallel those of B. S. Childs, who found that

> in the great majority of cases, the formula 'until this day' has been secondarily added as a redactional commentary on existing traditions[1].

Thus, even this widely accepted feature of etiological narrative turns out to be much less reliable as an identifier than previously assumed. Together, our results begin to show how elusive this category of marks really can be. One suspects that the locus of criteria commonly used to identify etiological narrative all along has been within the interpreter rather than the material itself.

The suspicion is not less grounded when one now looks at the manner in which sundry types of alleged etiological narrative have been reconstructed and posited as earlier stages of tradition now preserved in the Old Testament. Gunkel, for example, brilliantly and systematically employed what might be called an inferential model in reconstructing the "original sense" of many of the sagas in Genesis. Typical of his method is the treatment of Gen 19 1-28[2]. According to Gunkel, the historical impetus for the early form of the saga must have been the sight of utter desolation in the Dead Sea area. Whoever gazed on the scene would say, "Why has Yahweh done this to this land? What caused this fierce anger?" And then one would answer, "Therefore — because they have sinned against Yahweh — his anger burned against this land". The saga, then, was originally concerned with the origin of an unusual and surprising situation[3].

Obviously Gunkel has provided a methodological program for working within the classical definition of etiological narrative. One takes from a story an inference which reflects in some way a given historical circumstance ("Therefore, his anger burned against this land"), supposes this to be an answer to a previous question which originally gave rise to the entire tradition, and thereby understands

---

[1] JBL 82 (1963), 289f.

[2] Gunkel, Genesis, 215.

[3] The general lines of Gunkel's reconstruction have been widely accepted (though not unanimously), if one disregards the voluminous debate on the historicity of the catastrophe and its geographical location. Cf. for example, Driver, Genesis, 203, and Skinner, Genesis, 310ff.; von Rad, Genesis, 216, strongly suggests Gunkel's view; perhaps Speiser (Genesis 142) agrees in part.

the story itself as justification for the inference already supplied. Gunkel followed this program throughout his commentary on Genesis, and fathered the widespread reconstructions later made on quite diverse materials[4]. Recently, for example, Martin Noth has understood Jos 2 and 6 17b. 22. 23. 25 as a story which seeks to explain the presence of a "House of Rahab" (regarded as Canaanite) in the midst of Israel[5]. It is clear that he has implicitly imposed an inferential model on an extensive narrative which in fact contains no inferential statement. Indeed, Childs has argued that the phrase in Jos 6 25, "and she dwelt in Israel to this day", not only cannot be taken in an inferential sense, but relative to v. 17, must be secondary to the main tradition[6].

The more pervasive difficulty here, to which my work speaks, is that this inferential model is never actually attested with extensive narrative tradition. The obvious examples of the pattern in etymological materials have been shown to occur in short reports secondary or subordinate to the main dramatic movement of the wider context. At most and only two times at that, it appears in developed narratives anecdotal in length. There is no existent inferential model among etymological etiologies comparable, say, to the Rahab story, or the Sodom saga, in length and degree of literary development.

Furthermore, a study of those inferential clauses beginning with על־כן or לכן which deal with something other than etymology, and which show any possible link to etiological interests, leads to a similar conclusion.

1. על־כן (לכן) with a Qatal verb form

(a) I Sam 10 10-12 reports that Saul met a band of prophets at Gibeah and began to prophesy along with them. The spectators asked, among other things, "Is Saul also among the prophets?" From this report, the immediate inference is drawn:

על־כן היתה למשל
הגם שאול בנבאים

The impersonal formulation of the inference, the repetition of phraseology in the spectator's question and the proverbial saying, as well as the frequent use of the verb nb' and its related noun, show clearly that the whole piece functions analogously to a simple Form II etymological report. The narrative material surely intends to ground a

---

[4] Cf., for example, the program for exegesis of blessings such as are found in Gen 9 25ff. or 48 19ff.: "The goal of our exegesis of the blessing (i. e., 9 25ff.) must be to recognize the historical situation which the narrator has in view, and to understand the blessing itself as a naive explanation of the relationships of that time." Genesis 80. Cf. also 242 (Gen 22).

[5] M. Noth, Josua, 22 f.   [6] B. S. Childs, JBL 82 (1963), 286.

popular expression in a particular incident in Saul's rise to power.
The two verses, however, express at best a subordinate theme in the
larger context[7]. Indeed, v. 10-12 (13a) seem somewhat ill fitted to follow v. 9, which gives the impression of summarily ending an episode[8].
In any case, the fact that this etiology appears in chapter 19 in
quite another context indicates that it is only loosely rooted in specific narrative traditions about Saul, and thus is not likely to be
linked integrally to this account of Saul's annointing and the miraculous "signs".

(b) The closest formal parallel to this passage appears in Jos
14 14. Caleb pleas for possession of the hill country (14 6-12) and is
given Hebron as an inheritance (v. 13). A concluding remark immediately follows:

עד־היום הזה ... על־כן היתה־חברון לכלב
יען אשר מלא אחרי יהוה

Although similar in form to I Sam 10 12, this verse functions quite
differently. To be sure, the phrase "until this day" — whether modifying לנחלה or היתה ... לכלב — establishes a continuity into the
present of the narrator. In this respect, the clause seems to be an
inference whose truth is applicable in all time. Yet the על־כן clause
does not carry the same force here as it does in I Sam 10 12. The
latter derives a popular saying from a reported speech. Logically,
this means that a causal relationship between two states of affairs
is inferred, and given expression by על־כן. The effect is to bring a
new element (the proverb) into relation with an old (the speech) so
that the old provides a reason for the new. Now nothing of the sort
is going on in Jos 14 14. There is no inference of causality simply
because no new element is introduced. Verse 14, rather, summarizes
in almost identical words what has already been asserted in v. 13b.

Moreover, as Childs has noted, the verse in question reflects a
theological doctrine of the deuteronomist (cf. v. 9) who presupposes
a previously existing tradition (Num 13—14 Dtn 1 19ff.), and thus
cannot be forced into an etiological mold[9]. Finally, one should note
that the specific locale, Hebron, is not mentioned until the very end
of the episode extending over v. 6-14. This further confirms Child's
point that the interest lay elsewhere than in providing an explanation
of Caleb's claim to Hebron[10]. Thus Jos 14 14 does not function as an
etiology.

---

[7] Cf. Gressmann, Geschichtsschreibung, 26ff.; Hertzberg, I and II Samuel, 86. Cf.
also Smith, Samuel, 70.
[8] Cf. A. Weiser, Samuel: Seine geschichtliche Aufgabe und religiöse Bedeutung, 1962,
59.   [9] Childs, JBL 82 (1963), 287.
[10] Against Noth, Josua, 84.

(c) In the account of David's dealings with Achish (I Sam 27 1-7), a short tradition reports that Ziklag was given to David as a dwelling place (v. 5-6a). The inference is then drawn:

לכן היתה צקלג למלכי יהודה עד־היום הזה

Viewing the form of the whole, and the inferential function of the לכן clause, one is justified in seeing here an etiological form parallel to that in I Sam 10 10-12 and those of Form II etymological etiological reports. However, the phrase "Kings of Judah" only refers to monarchs of the period following the division of the kingdom. If v. 6b, then, were original to this tradition, the force of the anecdote would have been to explain a late monarchial claim on Ziklag. But in view of I Sam 30, where David's claim to this city is undisputed, such an original function for the tradition is neither necessary nor likely. Hence, the inference of ownership is probably secondary[11]. In any case, even if one were to judge v. 5-6 as integral etiological tradition, it comprises no more than a brief report.

(d) The remaining passages, although formally similar, and perhaps related distantly to etiological interests, functioned quite differently, and in various ways were disconnected from a narrative context:

(1) Motive clauses in legislation: Ex 20 11 Num 18 24
(2) Prescriptive speech: Lev 17 12
(3) Secondary material: Dtn 10 9a

(e) By way of summary, the על־כן inferential clause with Qatal verb form, exclusive of etymologies, functioned etiologically and integrally with narrative material only one time, i. e., I Sam 10 10-12. Perhaps there is a second example in I Sam 27 5-6. In no case was the inferential model associated with extensive narrative materials.

2. על־כן (לכן) with Yiqtal verb form

(a) Gen 10 9 reports that Nimrod was a mighty hunter before Yahweh. An inference is then drawn:

על־כן יאמר כנמרד גבור ציד לפני יהוה

The repetition of phraseology in v. 9a and 9b leave little doubt that the על־כן clause, formulated with an indefinite subject and to be translated, "it is said", functions integrally with brief narrative material. One sees here a simple report in two parts:

(1) Report
(2) Inference based directly on the report

---

[11] Childs op. cit. 287.
[12] Cf. the corrupt text in Gen 22 14b. Cf. above, 28f.

The structure obviously is analogous to a simple Form II etymological report, and to I Sam 10 10-12. The unit functions etiologically, that is, to explain the origin of a popular expression[12]. It is also clear that v. 9 is presently independent of any wider narrative context[13]. The report is simply one of several items in a series which preserves fragments of Nimrod traditions.

(b) A similar form is likely contained in II Sam 5 8. The text is very uncertain[14]. An על־כן clause, however, is clear in the latter half of the verse:

עַל־כֵּן יֹאמְרוּ עִוֵּר וּפִסֵּחַ לֹא יָבוֹא אֶל־הַבָּיִת

Since the third masculine plural has no obvious referent, the subject of the clause is indefinite, and most naturally translated as a general present: "they say" or "one says" or even "it is said . . ." The formulation is clearly parallel to the Niphal of Gen 10 9. Probably an inference is drawn from the narrated quote of v. 8a, as the repetition of עורים . . . הפסחים and עור ופסח indicates. It seems likely that the now obscure verse originally functioned to ground this particular restriction on blind and lame persons. Yet the connections with v. 6f. and 9 are very loose, and probably secondary. Verse 8 actually breaks the continuity between v. 7 and 9, and is chronologically out of place following a report of victory in v. 7. At most, therefore, v. 8 comprises a simple etiological report without demonstrable links to a developed narrative tradition.

(c) I Sam 19 18-24 provides an example of this fundamental report structure along with a more developed "story" context. There is clear dramatic movement in this piece. Saul sends one, two, three groups of messengers to capture David. Each prophesies. Finally Saul himself goes, and even he prophesies (v. 23. 24). From this dramatic resting point, the inference to a proverbial saying is directly drawn:

עַל־כֵּן יֹאמְרוּ הֲגַם שָׁאוּל בַּנְּבִיאִם

This conclusive clause is typically formulated with an indefinite subject. The consistent use of the verb nb' (v. 20. 21[2]. 23. 24) and emphatic גם המה or גם הוא (v. 20. 21[2]. 23. 24[2]), as well as the measured dramatic progression, indicate that these verses comprise an integral unit quite independent of its wider context[15]. The similarities with Form II etymological etiological narrative are obvious. Here the material —

---

[13] Gunkel, Genesis, 89; Holzinger, Genesis, 99; Skinner, Genesis, 208.

[14] Cf. Driver, Notes², 260 ff.

[15] On the literary criticism, cf. Gressmann, Geschichtsschreibung, 87 ff.; Nowack, Richter, Ruth . . . Samuelis, 100 ff.; Smith, Samuel, 181; Hertzberg, I and II Samuel, 167.

consisting of a two part form essentially unaltered from that of Gen 10 9 and II Sam 5 8 — functions etiologically to ground a popular saying in a particular event. However, even with this degree of literary complexity, the inferential structure includes narrative traditions merely of anecdotal length.

(d) The remaining examples of similar על־כן clauses, even though related to etymological interests, have lost any constitutive connections with narrative material, or have been secondarily added to previously existing traditions.

(1) Sundry concluding remarks, secondary to their contexts:
I Sam 5 5 and Gen 32 33[16]
Gen 2 24[17]

(2) Redactional linkage of independent tradition:
Num 21 14. 27[18]

These passages represent, therefore, a decadent stage in the history of this inferential structure.

(e) To summarize, the על־כן conclusive clause with a Yiqtal verb form, exclusive of etymological material, functioned etiologically and integrally with narrative tradition in a way which was analogous to the pattern of Form II etymological reports. The clause was used to ground proverbial sayings (I Sam 19 24 II Sam 5 8 Num 21 27 Gen 10 9), cultic practices (Gen 32 33 I Sam 5 5), and a biological phenomenon (Gen 2 24). In only one case was there a developed "story" context integrally related to the inference (I Sam 19 18-24). Even here, the material was anecdotal in length. Thus, there is no attested example of the inferential model being integrally associated with extensive narrative tradition.

In the light of these conclusions, the pervasive difficulty in the usual reconstruction or identification of alleged etiological narrative is brought into sharp focus. The inferential model commonly employ-

---

[16] Cf. Childs, JBL 82 (1963), 287f. Gen 32 33 is interesting because it offers the only example, exclusive of etymological material, of a *kî* explanatory clause giving the grounds for the etiological inference. One may suppose that the form of this verse is influenced by the etymological pattern occasionally observed (e. g., Gen 11 9).

[17] Opinions differ as to whether or not v. 24 represents a secondary layer in the tradition. The analysis of the etymological elements (cf. above, 53f.) tends to indicate its independence of the structure of v. 18-23. Moreover, the dramatic movement from tension (no helpmate) to resolution (a helpmate is finally created) does not directly motivate the inference made in v. 24. The latter in my opinion, goes in quite a surprising direction. In any case, the narrative tradition in question is hardly more than anecdotal in length.

[18] Cf. Gressmann, Anfänge, 113f. and 116f.; Holzinger, Numeri, 95 and 99f.; Gray, Numbers, 294 and 299.

ed is never attested with extensive narrative tradition, and only rarely with relatively developed story material anecdotal in length. It is with doubtful justification, therefore, that an inferential model, explicitly or implicitly, can be used in discussing extensively developed traditions as alleged etiological narrative. To do so involves an unwarranted assumption of a breadth of applicability simply unattested in the Old Testament texts. If the inferential structure ever shaped an extensive "story" tradition, it is odd indeed that nothing of this has survived. It seems more likely — in view of the copious examples of short reports — that this particular model, or better, creative mold, never achieved the formative power necessary to provide the focus for narrative traditions of greater complexity than anecdotes similar to Gen 11 1-9 or I Sam 19 18-24.

If this is correct, then those instances where the inferential model is operative, e. g., etymologies of the Form II type and certain others, most of which involve proverbial sayings, ought to be separated clearly from that large body of narrative material which does not conform to the pattern. The question is still open if the latter be etiological, how the material actually functions, and what its identifying marks might be. It only confuses matters, however, to assume a homogeneity of form and function where none exists.

The evidence marshalled, then, limits somewhat the current discussion of etiological narrative. But it also points toward an area of further investigation. The problem now, if one continues to focus upon marks, is to devise a methodology which will yield results in those cases of alleged etiological tradition where no clear formula or inferential structure is apparent. Briefly, the question is: are there distinctive signs in *this* material which show it to function etiologically? An answer may require a broader approach. That is, a wider knowledge of the various marks which reveal a story's function is needed to bring a measure of control to the diverse literature. If such devices can be isolated and identified as conventional aspects of an Israelitic narrative art, then important criteria will have been gained for the examination of Hebrew stories, always done, of course, in light of their various stages of growth. Perhaps then one can begin to speak a little more assuredly of an etiological function for a given narrative[19].

---

[19] Among form critics, this sort of broadly based research which strives for a high degree of precision, has only recently begun to appear. Cf. W. Richter, Untersuchungen, especially 344 ff. Cf. also L. Alonso-Schökel, Erzählkunst im Buche der Richter, Biblica 42 (1961), 143—172.

BEIHEFTE ZUR ZEITSCHRIFT
FÜR DIE ALTTESTAMENTLICHE WISSENSCHAFT

Herausgegeben von GEORG FOHRER

Lieferungsmöglichkeiten und Preise der früheren Hefte auf Anfrage

VERLAG ALFRED TÖPELMANN · BERLIN 30

August Freiherr von Gall

Der hebräische Pentateuch der Samaritaner
5 Teile

I. Teil: Prolegomena und Genesis. Mit 4 Tafeln. — II. Teil: Exodus.
III. Teil: Leviticus. — IV. Teil: Numeri. — V. Teil: Deuteronomium nebst
Nachträgen und Verbesserungen
Quart. XVI, XCIV, 440 Seiten. 1914/1918. Nachdruck 1966. Ganzleinen DM 110,—

Mark Lidzbarski

Ephemeris für semitische Epigraphik
3 Bände. Groß-Oktav

I. Band: 1900—1902. Mit 49 Abbildungen. — IV, 371 Seiten. — II. Band: 1903—1907.
Mit 1 Schrifttafel und 38 Abbildungen. VIII, 444 Seiten. — III. Band 1909—1915.
Mit 15 Tafeln und 107 Abbildungen im Text. VI, 322 Seiten.
Halbleder DM 300,—

Mark Lidzbarski

Das Johannesbuch der Mandäer
2 Teile

I. Teil: Text. — II. Teil: Einleitung, Übersetzung, Kommentar.
Groß-Oktav. XXXVI, 256, 291 Seiten. 1905—1915. Nachdruck 1966.
Ganzleinen DM 110,—

Adolf Erman

Die Religion der Ägypter
Ihr Werden und Vergehen in 4 Jahrtausenden

Mit 10 Tafeln und 186 Abbildungen. Oktav. XVI, 483 Seiten. 1934.
Nachdruck 1968. Mit einem Nachwort von Eberhard Otto. Ganzleinen DM 48,—

Johannes Hempel

Die althebräische Literatur
und ihr hellenistisch-jüdisches Nachleben

Quart. IV, 203 Seiten. Mit 71 Abbildungen und 6 Tafeln. 1930.
Nachdruck 1968. Ganzleinen DM 36,—

WALTER DE GRUYTER & CO · BERLIN 30